✠

Memorias de mi viaje/
Recollections of My Trip

✠

Olga Beatriz Torres

Translated by Juanita Luna-Lawhn

Originally Published by *El Paso del Norte*, El Paso, Texas, 1918
University of New Mexico Press
Albuquerque

Library of Congress Cataloging-in-Publication Data

Torres, Olga Beatriz.
Memorias de mi viaje = Recollections of my trip / by Olga Beatriz
Torres ; translated by Juanita Luna-Lawhn. — 1st ed.
p. cm.
"Originally published by El Paso del Norte, El Paso, Texas, 1918."
Spanish and English.
Includes bibliographical references and index.
ISBN 0–8263–1532–1
1. Torres, Olga Beatriz—Correspondence. 2. Texas—Description
and travel. 3. Mexican American women—Texas—Correspondence.
4. Mexican Americans—Texas—Correspondence. 5. Refugees—Texas—
Correspondence. I. Luna-Lawhn, Juanita. II. Title. III. Title: Recollections of my trip.
F395.M5T67   1994
917.6404´61—dc20   94–21543
[B]   CIP

I dedicate this book to my brothers,
Pablo Severo, Jesus, Luis, Juan, and Joe,
men of courage.

✛ CONTENTS ✛

✛ Preface ✛

The study of literature should be more than the hermetic conversation among pedantic academics that it seems to have become, even in—or perhaps better said, especially in—Chicano circles. In concrete terms, at its best, criticism opens a space of experience previously closed to us, unknown and, therefore, for our practical purposes, nonexistent. This function it shares with literature: as an act of creative writing, criticism tenders us a possibility of expanding life to where a moment before there seemed to be not only nothing worth pursuing, but no place at all. When a work that achieves this end falls into your hands, the thrill of discovery is its own reward. Just this kind of book is what you—by design or fortunate chance—have now begun to explore.

Professor Lawhn explains in her introduction how over the years she has researched the Generación del México de Afuera, the Mexican exile writers who fled the revolutionary turmoil during the first quarter of this century to find refuge, like countless displaced persons from all over the world, in the United States. And like so many of those exiles, the México de Afuera group prided itself on having maintained the authenticity of its Mexican culture, keeping in perfect tack through the constant practice of customs of the old country. In spite of residing in the United States, they considered themselves Mexicans, no different from their brethren who had remained behind. They represented their imaginary community as Mexican to the core.

The protagonists of this group were men, although women participated, relegated to marginal areas such as the women's pages or secretarial labor. For years no one questioned this gender monopoly, because it differed little from the general state of society everywhere and always—or at least as we were trained to think of it before feminist critics began to alter our perception of normality. Professor Lawhn, however, was disturbed by what to most seemed the natural state of things. As we worked side by side, squinting at the mind-numbing glare of microfilm screens, she would intone what became the leitmotif of the research: where were the women? Her question, of course, is the archetypal feminist inquiry, from which springs what has imposed itself as the most dynamic line of critical renovation in contemporary cultural studies.

To the patriarchal assertion that there were no women writers, Lawhn responded by finding Olga Beatriz Torres. Then, she set out to make the text available, translating it for the English reading public. But her work, of necessity, goes beyond discovery and promotion, because the reader's first reaction to the thin text could well be that it offers little of interest, that nothing special happens, and, worse, that the seemingly direct writing is of no particular significance. True, the text is sparse, simple, somewhat like a first draft of what might have been a more developed and fleshed-out text had the author been encouraged to rewrite—that is, had editors taken a serious interest in her work. That they would have if the text had been by a man we will never know, but perhaps. Yet Professor Lawhn refuses to allow the work to be dismissed or once again given short shrift. She determinedly makes us see what to her is obvious: this simple story contains the paradigm of the Mexican immigrant experience, the movement across political borders that produces, almost despite the immigrant's conscious intentions, a new, hybrid being, what we now call a Chicano/Chicana. Moreover, she purposefully positions Torres's story of cultural accommodation and fusion in direct opposition to the ideology of cultural resistance espoused by Torres's male contemporaries in the

México de Afuera generation—and later by the Américo Paredes school of cultural conflict—revealing a situation of intragroup dissent that undermines the position of both elitist and populist ideologues. It is remarkable how Torres's apparently simple tale, culminating as it does in the networking of women of different classes across the supposed divide between oral and written expression, belies the image of the border as resistance and separation, ending instead in the presence of the ongoing process of interlingual synthesis.

We are indebted to Professor Lawhn for this new opening in Chicano/Chicana literary space.

Bruce-Novoa

✛ Acknowledgments ✛

In the Spring of 1980, I met Professor Bruce-Novoa, who, at the time, was researching the life and literary production of Martín Luis Guzmán. That year we reviewed countless microfilm reels of *La Prensa* of San Antonio to confirm that several of Martín Luis Guzmán's novels had been serialized in *La Prensa* during the 1920s. As we worked, I vocalized my concern over the lack of literary contributions by women in the newspaper. As a response to my concern and interest in Mexican women publishing in the United States during the turn of the century, I began to compile a bibliography of women who had been published in *La Prensa*. This effort led me to locate several books published in Texas by women of El México de Afuera. One of these texts is Olga Beatriz Torres's *Memorias de mi viaje* (*Recollections of My Trip*).

There have been many persons, colleagues and family members, who have contributed to my success in translating the text and in getting my translation ready for publication. I take this opportunity to thank all those who so graciously gave me their time, patience, and love. First, I want to thank my husband, James, for his support, for not questioning my long hours of work, and for keeping the computer going. Without his computer expertise, I would never have been able to complete the text as quickly as I have. I also want to thank Jaime Luis, my son, for supporting my work and reassuring me that I would be able to meet my deadline; my sisters, Estella, Margaret, Candida, María Isabel, and mother and father, Natividad C. and Pablo H. Luna, for educating me; Professor Bruce-Novoa for encouraging me to work on the literature of women of the Texas border; Don Luis Leal for saying during the 1986 NEH Summer Seminar, "Siga buscando allí en Texas"; Professor Rebolledo, my friend, for introducing me to Andrea Otañez, editor of the University of New Mexico Press and for reading my manuscript; Andrea Otañez for supporting the work of women; Professor Ellen Shull of Palo Alto College and Professor Isabel Jennings of San Antonio College for reading my manuscript; and Margarita T. Rivera for being my friend and reading the initial version of the translation. I also want to thank San Antonio College for supporting my work, in particular, the Faculty Development Program, which has funded several grants to work on *La Prensa*, and the Learning Resource Center librarians for their support during my long hours of research. Finally, I want to thank my colleagues of the English Department at San Antonio College for providing the support necessary to continue my professional growth.

Memorias de mi viaje/ Recollections of My Trip

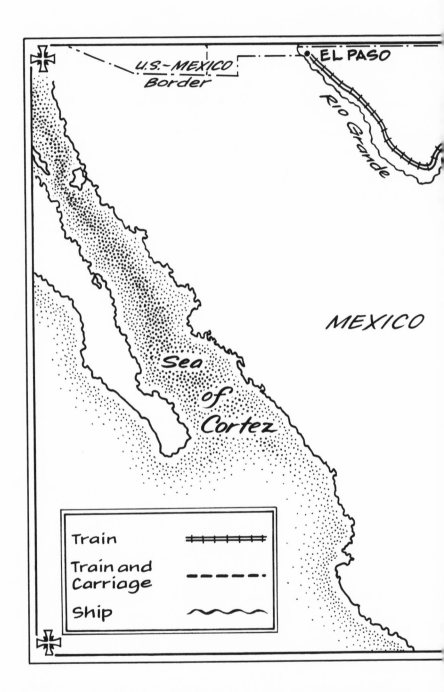

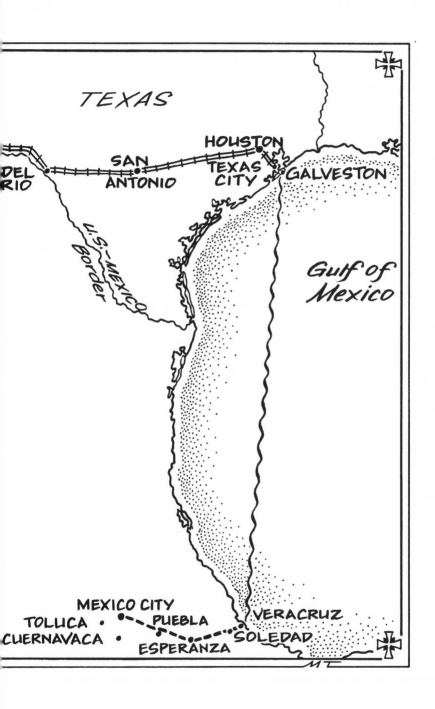

✠ *MEMORIAS DE MI VIAJE* (*RECOLLECTIONS OF MY TRIP*): A TRANSCULTURAL VOYAGE INTO EL MÉXICO DE AFUERA ✠

During the period 1910–20, the United States experienced an influx of Mexican exiles who crossed the U.S.-Mexican border into the Southwest to seek refuge from political persecution or to escape the internal and political turmoil created and fermented by the Mexican Revolution.[1] It was during this period that Rodolfo Uranga, then an expatriate living in San Antonio and writing for *La Prensa* of San Antonio, Texas, coined the term *El México de Afuera*, those living outside Mexico, to define this group of Mexican exiles.[2] Although many of the exiles settled along the border towns of New Mexico, Arizona, California, and Texas, many continued their migration into the states of Kansas, Colorado, Indiana, Ohio, Illinois, and Michigan.[3] The community of exiles soon came to be identified as El México de Afuera, and when the financially and intellectually elite members of the group settled in San Antonio, as they did in other cities across the United States, they created their own separate community known as the *colonia mexicana*.

In his 1940 chapbook *El México de Afuera: y su reintegración a la patria*, Fedérico Allen Hinojosa amplified Uranga's definition of the members of El México de Afuera.[4] Hinojosa characterized members of the *colonia mexicana* as Mexican exiles who (1) left Mexico to escape the internal turmoil of the Mexican Revolution and possessed a determined and unyielding nationalistic spirit; (2) yearned for the day when they would return to a unified and prosperous mother country; (3) celebrated annual patriotic festivals in which they paid homage to Mexican heroes such as Benito Juárez and Miguel Hidalgo; (4) retained their Mexican citizenship as well as their Mexican culture; (5) maintained their Catholic religion with a strong love and veneration for the Virgen de Guadalupe, an extension of their love and veneration for the Virgen de Tepeyac; (6) retained their Spanish language; and (7) considered themselves as having spiritually reconquered Mexican territories lost in 1837 and 1847 to the United States.[5]

Because the *colonia mexicana* was by nature nationalistic, it developed on the periphery of the Anglo community. The Texas Mexican community maintained and sustained itself as self-sufficient and self-governing, and as a result, many of the Mexican exiles became a major force in making their community independent. They started businesses, were involved in broadcasting, selected and presented social and theatrical performances that reinforced their cultural nationalism, created medical clinics, defended the legal rights of their members, established and participated in social and political organizations,[6] and created a strong literary circle, which I have chosen to refer to as the *Generation of El México de Afuera*, as suggested by Professor Luis Leal of the University of California at Santa Barbara.

In San Antonio, the leading members of the literary group were Ignacio E. Lozano, the leader often referred to as the educator of El México de Afuera; Nemesio García Naranjo; Guillermo Aguirre y Fierro; José I. Rebollar; Fedérico Allen Hinojosa; Teodoro Torres, Jr.; Manuel Muzquiz Blanco; Alfredo González; and Alfonso Anaya. Although there were not many women involved in the literary group, Rosario Sansores, Hortensia Elizondo, and Beatriz Blanco, women who contributed regularly to *La Prensa*, can be considered members of the circle.

After settling in the United States, many of the members who had been journalists in Mexico created their own newspaper enterprises or worked as journalists in the Spanish-language newspapers of the Southwest. In San Antonio, Texas, for example, Ignacio E. Lozano founded *La Prensa*, the most influential newspaper for El México de Afuera; Nemesio García Naranjo edited *Revista Mexicana* from August 1915 to January 1920; Guillermo Aguirre y Fierro edited the weekly *Chiltipiquin* from 1914–15; from October 1914 to July 1915, Arturo Elías and Luis Medina published the weekly *El Presidente;* in 1919, José Rebollar edited the weekly *El Trabajo;* and in 1934,[7] Beatriz Blanco edited *El Album de la Raza.*

Many of the newspapers of El México de Afuera also created their own publishing houses and printed the literary works of Latin American writers, translations of major and minor European writers, and works written by their own literary group. Although the themes of the books they published varied, in the 1920s, the publishing house Casa Editorial Lozano published a series of novels whose authors developed their plots around the theme of the Mexican Revolution. Among these novels were *El automóvil gris* (1922) and *Heraclio Bernal: el Rayo de Sinoloa* (1920) by José Asención Reyes, *Pancho Villa: una vida de romance y tragedia* (1924) by Teodoro Torres, *!Ladrona¡* (1925) by Miguel Arce, *Carranza* (1928) by Alfredo González,[8] and the serialized novels of Martín Luis Guzmán in *La Prensa.*[9] Unfortunately, even though women such as Rosario Sansores, Hortencia Elizondo, and Beatriz Blanco served in the editorial board of *La Prensa*, my research has not located any novels written by these women. Because their journalistic pieces in *La Prensa* were not political nor concerned with the subject of the Mexican Revolution, their beliefs, attitudes, and political agendas concerning the Mexican Revolution remain absent from the El México de Afuera body of literature. As a result, until the recent discovery of Olga Beatriz Torres's epistolary memoir *Memorias de mi viaje*, the study of the ideology of El México de Afuera had been limited to the views presented by its male writers.

Because many México de Afuera writers intended to return to Mexico, it is often difficult to locate biographical data on them. Such is the case with Olga Beatriz Torres. At this time, the only information I have been able to locate is that she came from Villa Olga, near Mexico City, with her parents and two sisters, and that her father's name was Julian. Searches of the Texas census records for 1910 and 1920 have not revealed further information. As I continue to research El México de Afuera, it is possible that I will locate additional biographical data on Olga Beatriz Torres.

As a member of the Generation of El México de Afuera, Olga Beatriz Torres's work is one of the few literary pieces that reveals the psychological impact of transculturalization, for as Torres's text tracks the movement from one culture to another, it demonstrates the narrator's psychological response to that movement—that is, her movement away from Mexican culture and into U.S. culture. Torres's epistolary memoir was serialized and published by *El Paso del Norte*, a México de Afuera newspaper edited by Fernando Gamiochipi that distinguished itself as "the only Constitutional daily of El Paso, Texas, written by Mexicans." *El Paso del Norte* identified itself with the forces and ideas of Venustiano Carranza.[10] The copy of the text I have translated and used for this study was Silvestre Terrazas's personal copy, sent to him by Torres. A short note written by Olga Beatriz inside the text illustrates Torres's respect for and friendship with the editor of *La Patria* in Chihuahua. Because Terrazas was also an important editor of another México de Afuera newspaper, *La Patria*, of El Paso, Texas, when he lived in Texas,[11] Olga's note is significant, because it illustrates that she communicated and had professional contact with other literary members of El México de Afuera.

It is also worth noting that Torres's work was first serialized in *El Paso del Norte*, the newspaper that in 1915 serialized Mariano Azuela's novel, *Los de abajo*, one of the first, and still most read, novels of the Mexican Revolution.[12] However, I have been unable to document the exact date or dates that Torres's work appeared in the newspaper,

A Transcultural Voyage

because a complete microfilm copy of *El Paso del Norte* is unavailable in the United States. Thus, I can not confirm whether Torres's letters appeared before, during, or after the 1915 serialized version of Azuela's *Los de abajo*. I can, however, infer from the text that the travels of Olga Beatriz Torres occurred during the summer of 1914, the year the United States occupied the port of Veracruz, and that the publication of the text in book form was in 1918. Thus, Torres's letter to her Tía Ciria in Mexico appeared in *El Paso del Norte* between 1914 and 1918. The discovery of Torres's text expands the body of literature written and published in the United States by Mexicans living outside Mexico during the Mexican Revolution. More important, it provides a feminine perspective to the Mexican Revolution, one that permits the reader to examine the ideology of El México de Afuera from a female viewpoint.

While in the United States, El México de Afuera newspaper editors used Spanish-language newspapers to strengthen solidarity among the Mexican community. In its twentieth year of publication, the editors of *La Prensa* printed an editorial, "Veinte Años de Vida," that restated and reaffirmed the philosophy of the newspaper and, in essence, the ideology of El México de Afuera. It stated that

> nuestro programa, sencillo y amplio a la vez, se encierra en esta sola frase: servir a México y a los mexicanos y honrar a la Patria en cuantas ocasiones tengamos oportunidad de hacerlo . . . como médula de la publicación, una tesis invariable que pregona el engrandecimiento de México, la armonía de la gran familia mexicana, la consolidación de los más puros ideales patrióticos por medio de la libertad y del orden . . . Por último, en país extranjero, donde con tanta facilidad el idioma se corrompe y desvirtúa, contaminándose de impropios o francamente disparatados, *La Prensa* ha procurado mantener con limpieza la lengua castellana, que es la de México, convencidos de que el lenguaje es uno de los baluartes más sólidos de la cultura patria, y, por lo tanto, de la nacionalidad.[13]

[Our program, uncomplicated, but at the same time, extensive, is encapsuled in the following sentence: to serve Mexico and Mexicans and to honor our land wherever and whenever we have the opportunity to do so . . . the crux of the paper, an invariable thesis that heralds the exaltation of Mexico, the harmony of the strong Mexican family, the consolidation of the purest patriarchal ideals via freedom and order . . . Finally, in a foreign land, where a language can be easily corrupted and adulterated, contaminated by improper words or, frankly, just poppycock, *La Prensa* has endeavored to maintain pure the Castilian language, the language of Mexico, convinced that the language is one of the strongest bastions of our Nation's culture, and, therefore, of our nationality.]

It is evident that the patriarchal ideology of El México de Afuera sought to maintain itself culturally intact and to protect itself, as much as possible, from the contamination of U.S. culture, an act practiced and proven effective by maintaining the Spanish language pure and free from the linguistic influences of English.

Ironically, in 1933 the Mexican press accused the México de Afuera press of having assimilated into U.S. culture. A Mexico City daily referred to *La Prensa* as a foreign and "Yankee" paper. For a patriotic and nationalistic community like El México de Afuera, this designation was an affront, and on 1 August 1933, the editors of *La Prensa* responded with their editorial titled "Los Sentires de Este México."[14] The editors explained:

Primero, sólo para ir por orden, diremos que los Periódicos Lozano no son "publicaciones extranjeras." Primero, porque desde la dirección hasta el último puesto, somos netamente mexicanos. Luego, porque la ideología de estas publicaciones es absolutamente, profundamente mexicana; y finalmente, porque sus páginas están dedicadas única y exclusivamente a los lectores mexicanos e hispano americanos, que por diversas circunstancias

A Transcultural Voyage

residen en este lado del Río Grande. Y esto es muy simple demostrarlo, con sólo hojear cualquier ejemplar de estas publicaciones... Los mexicanos que viven en los Estados Unidos, siguen vibrando, sintiendo, pensando, como los mexicanos que no han salido de su patria. En sus mentes está siempre la esperanza del retorno, tarde o temprano. En suelo extranjero, las colonias mexicanas continúan rindiendo culto a sus próceres, celebrando las fechas consagradas por la tradición, manteniendo viva en el espíritu de sus hijos la lámpara votiva ante el altar de la Patria. No se han desligado de los asuntos de México, qué les atañen personalmente, ya que no han perdido ni su nombre, ni su idioma, ni su nacionalidad . . .'[15]

[First, just to keep things straight, the Lozano papers are not "foreign publications." . . . First of all, all jobs necessary to produce a newspaper are held by Mexicans. Then, the ideology of the publication is absolutely and profoundly Mexican; and finally, the paper is directed exclusively to a Mexican and Hispanic American reading public who because of diverse circumstances reside on this side of the Rio Grande . . . Mexicans who live in the United States continue to breathe, feel, and think like Mexicans who have not had to leave their country. The hope, the desire to return to Mexico is always present in the minds of those living outside of Mexico. In a foreign land, the *colonias mexicanas* continue to demonstrate their loyalty to their predecessors, celebrate traditional holidays, and teach their children to remain loyal to their homeland. They do not separate from nor forget to remain in contact with the daily occurrences of Mexico. They have not lost their names, their language, nor their citizenship . . .]

The editors further challenged the editor of the Mexico City newspaper to visit and observe that Mexicans living in the United States had remained Mexicans. He stated:

Si los compatriotas que residen en México y nos desconocen— entre ellos el editorialista a que aludimos en este artículo—se dieran una vuelta por acá antes de emitir sus juicios, de un simple vistazo palparían la importancia y el sentir del "México de Afuera," y de la verdadera significación de estos periodicos.[16]

[If our countrymen who reside in Mexico and who do not recognize us any longer—among them the editor that we allude to in this editorial—would come to the United States before they express their biased opinions and take a quick look, they would realize the importance and the convictions of "El México de Afuera" and the true significance of these newspapers.]

Ironically, as much as the patriarchy of El México de Afuera wanted to remain Mexican and culturally pure, Olga Beatriz Torres's epistolary work illustrates that once a Mexican crossed the border into the United States, the process of transculturalization was initiated and remaining "culturally pure" (i.e., Mexican) was, and is, almost an impossibility.

Torres's journey into the United States began on 28 June 1914, at 4:30 A.M., from Villa Olga, Mixcoac, a village twenty minutes outside Mexico City. As Torres begins her travel, she experiences the foreboding sensation of loss. First, she sees the image of her village disappear into the trees. She states, "Ví `la Villa Olga,' mi casa querida, perderse entre el tupido cortinaje de los árboles."[17] ("I saw `Villa Olga,' my beloved home, lost amidst the density of the trees.") Second, while in Mexico City, she loses her voice. She relates, "Nos metimos al Pullman; yo no podía hablar ¿alegria? ¿tristeza? quizá las dos cosas . . ."[18] ("We boarded the Pullman. I was speechless. Joy? Sadness? Maybe both.") Third, when she is transferred to a military train, she loses her watch, which had been engraved with her initials. The disappearance of her home, her voice, and her engraved watch suggests the loss of the social code that orients her in her native land. Thus, the journey into a foreign land is a journey into the transformation of the self—a task that is accomplished by learning a totally new code, a new system of values, and a new language.

A Transcultural Voyage

From the center and capital of Mexico, Mexico City, Olga moves toward the national border, Veracruz. In the port of Veracruz, she comes in contact with the American soldier— evidence of the U.S. presence in Mexico. She laments the destruction of property caused by the American invasion of Veracruz. As Olga awaits for the ship that will take her to the United States, she sees American soldiers exploited by Mexican vendors, learns that the American military values hygiene, and abhors the Americans' monorhythmic military music. Finally, the ship, *City of Mexico*, that will transport the Mexican exiles, arrives in Veracruz. The ship's name appears in English and within quotation marks in the original version.[19] Of course, the ship is evidence of U.S. intervention in the transportation of Mexican exiles to the United States, an act that may not be totally accepted by all who take advantage of the service. Olga's father, for example, abhors the idea that he is seeking refuge in the United States. He states, "'Soldados Americanos' contestó mi papá y agregó emocionado `es triste verse obligado por la tiranía a buscar bajo el amparo de estos hombres paz y seguridad."[20] ("'American soldiers' answered my father and added emotionally, `It is sad that tyranny has obliged me to seek sanctuary among these men.'") When translated, the ship's name becomes *La ciudad de México*. Metaphorically, the ship becomes a floating microcosm of the *colonia mexicana* in the United States.

Like the ideology of El México de Afuera, Olga remains loyal to Mexico, as evidenced by her description of the ship:

> Orgullosa de haber nacido en la capital de la República, desearía que todo aquello que lleva su nombre, fuera grande y bello como es ella, pero el barco "City of México," es una solemne porquería que deshonra el nombre.[21]
>
> [Proud to have been born in the capitol of the Republic, I wish that everything that carries its name would be as big and as

beautiful as she is, but the ship "City of Mexico" is an utter piece of junk that dishonors the name.]

Significantly, when Olga describes the dining area of the ship, she begins to incorporate English into her sentences: "Some cabins open into the dining room which makes me believe that the dining area used to be a **hall**." As the ship moves across the Gulf, Olga experiences seasickness and becomes lightheaded and disoriented, a condition experienced by many of the passengers traveling to the United States. Symbolically, the disorientation is significant, because as Olga crosses the Gulf, she moves away from a familiar culture and language and toward a foreign culture and language.

After three days of being confined to her cabin, Olga returns to the deck, begins to meet other passengers, and initiates her integration into the community of El México de Afuera. She acknowledges the people traveling with her and her family. Among the passengers are two nuns, one from Catalonia and the other from the United States. Olga states:

> Figúrate: dos monjas teresianas, una ya grande, catalana y la otra americana; pero hija de padres mexicanos; iban para San Antonio, Texas, como profesoras de un colegio católico: la muchacha iba además a ver a sus padres, que desde hacía cuatro años no los veía, parte de cuyo tiempo pasó en el Colegio Teresiano de Mixcoac.[22]
>
> [Imagine two St. Teresa nuns, an older catalonian and an American, but of Mexican parents; they were going to San Antonio, Texas, as professors of a Catholic school. The girl was also going to see her parents whom she had not seen in four years since she had lived at St. Teresa College in Mixcoac.]

It is on the ship that Olga first comes in contact with what we would today call a Chicana. Olga uses the term *mexicano* or *mexicana* to refer to an individual born in the United States but of Mexican heritage.

In addition, there was a rich Mexican family, a Japanese captain, and an American family, the Newmans.

On 7 July, the ship reaches Texas City, where the passengers are not permitted to disembark until they are vaccinated and the ship is fumigated. This is the second time that the passengers are vaccinated, the first vaccination having taken place in the military train when she was en route to the port of Veracruz. Olga's attention is drawn once again to the emphasis placed on hygiene, a value that emerges out of the fear of contamination. She had experienced it as a cultural value associated with the United States in Veracruz when she noted that the city was extraordinarily clean because the U.S. military captain stationed in the city had ordered a thorough cleanup. Olga learns that before people can disembark from the ship and step on U.S. soil, they must be interrogated by an immigration agent and prove that they are financially stable, hard workers, and of "good breeding." Olga says, "¡Aquí consideran a los pobres tan peligrosos como a los enfermos contagiosos!"[23] ("Here the poor are considered as dangerous as those with a contagious disease.")

Finally, when Olga is permitted to leave the ship, she experiences the first disappointment:

> Llegamos a la primera, frente al paradero de los trenes eléctricos, y mi desencanto fué mayor: figúrate un jacalón de madera que con divisiones interiores era a la vez habitación y tienda: . . . y aquel "establecimiento" propiedad, entre parentesis de un mexicano casado con una alemana, era todo lo que de edificios había por allí.[24]
>
> [We arrived at the first one, in front of the electric train station, and my disillusionment was great; imagine a wooden shack with interior divisions which make it into a home and store at the same time; . . . and that "establishment," property, between parenthesis, of a Mexican married to a German woman was the only building in sight.]

Because Olga comes from a well-to-do family and is familiar with Mexico City, a major world capital with newly built train stations, she cannot fathom the humble buildings that she first comes in contact with in the United States.

Once in Texas, Olga starts her movement inland and increases her initiation into U.S. culture. As she boards a train to Houston, she finds that some of the seats in the back of the car are empty, and she and a Mexican woman take advantage of them. Soon after, one of the conductors speaks to her in English and points toward the For Colored sign hanging over the seat. Because Olga does not read English, her father translates for her what the conductor is ordering, and she moves to the front of the car.

Once in Houston, she tours the city. She takes "Main Street" and sees the Rice Hotel, Bristol Hotel, First National Bank, and post office. She characterizes the architecture by its sameness:

> Te diré: casi todos los edificios son de monótona arquitectura, son enormes moles cuadradas, salpicadas de ventanas rectangulares, que me hacen pensar en palomares gigantescos, sin arte alguno o, sin belleza de ninguna clase . . .[25]
>
> [I will tell you that almost all the buildings are made of a monotonous architecture. They are gigantic square masses sprinkled with rectangular windows that make me think of gigantic pigeon houses, without art or beauty of any kind . . .]

She also visits the rich neighborhoods of Houston and is pleased with their extravagance. Olga devotes a complete letter to Rice University and notes that it is coed. She states that women can study whatever they wish—even law, medicine, or engineering. The English language is interspersed throughout; "City Park" and "Main Street" are integrated into the letter. It is also interesting to note that whereas earlier she did not understand the For Colored sign, at this point, she sees and understands a sign in English that reads "Watermelons five cents a slice." She writes its Spanish translation in parentheses. As Olga begins her move inland toward the center of the state, she acquires more English and incorporates it into her letters to her aunt. She writes,

> Pasamos por la Corte ("**Court House**") que es el lugar de los tribunales, edificio muy bonito que rompe la monotonía de las demás casas, y seguimos por otras calles hasta entrar de nuevo a la "**Market Street**" (*Calle del mercado*) en donde, frente a una nevería, abandonamos el automóvil . . .[26]
>
> [We went by the Court House (**Court House**) which is the tribunal, a beautiful building that breaks the monotony of the rest of the buildings and continued through other streets until we again entered (**Market Street**) (Calle del mercado), where we got off the automobile in front of an ice cream parlor.]

In the original text, Olga uses the Spanish terms in the first part of the sentence and provides the English translation in parentheses. In the second half of the sentence, however, Olga uses the English words "Market Street" and gives the Spanish equivalent in parentheses. At this point, Olga's text demonstrates the genesis of code switching from Spanish and English and vice versa.

As Olga tours the inner city of Houston, she again comes in contact with the black community. Her attitudes were clearly shaped by an upper-class Mexican background that favored lighter skin, although in Mexico the prejudice was against Indians. Although she observes the horrible conditions in which they live, she accepts the segregation policy of the United States and is unsympathetic to their plight. In fact, she states,

> Son estos prójimos gente tan fea y tan sucia, que hacen bien los americanos de segregarlos de todo centro de blancos; y la segregración llega a grado tal, que aquí y en general en todo el

Estado de Texas, es un delito que un negro se case con una blanca o un blanco con una negra; de manera que además de declararse nulo el matrimonio, los contrayentes son puestos en la cárcel y severamente castigados.[27]

[These people are so ugly and dirty that Americans are right to segregate them from all white public places, and the segregation goes so far that in the state of Texas, it is a crime for a Negro man to marry a white woman or a white man to marry a Negro woman. In addition to declaring the marriage null and void, offenders are jailed and severely punished.]

Olga nevertheless continues to define the black community as a hardworking community that serves the white community well and as a group of people who consider the whites superior to them. Furthermore, she relates how most blacks work in fields and introduces the issue of the displacement of Negro labor in agriculture by the *mexicano*.

Olga finally reaches El Paso. She orients herself and again tours the city. As she has done before, whenever she sightsees, she buys a set of postcards of the city, because she believes that all important sites are photographed and sold as postcards. Postcards become her tour guide.

When she tours El Paso, she sees the Anson Mills building. She reads the English inscription posted at the entrance to the building, which notes that it was built on the site of the first Spanish settlement in Texas. Olga integrates the English inscription into her letter: "On this spot then—near the river—opposite the ancient—City of Paso del Norte—Juan María Ponce de Leon—the first settler—on this side built this house in 1827."[28] Olga indicates that the explanation to the text is included in a footnote, and the footnote appears at the bottom of the page. Just as the Spanish settlement displaced the English building, so English supplants the Spanish language in Olga's text.

As Olga moves to the center of Texas, and then north and west to El Paso, the process of transculturalization becomes more evident, particularly in the language of the last letter. Significantly, the greeting is replaced by the complete sentence, "Nos instalamos," which means "we installed ourselves" or "we established ourselves."[29] Metaphorically, this statement illustrates that the movement from Mexico City to El Paso, Texas, is complete. Olga and her family have reached their destination, and they resume a settled state by literally putting their things and themselves in place, away, signaling that they are no longer in transit.

Olga's journey is complete and her transculturalization is well under way, as evidenced by the architecture of her home and the language she uses to describe it: "Nuestra casa era un juguete, estilo misión, acabado de hacer: cinco piezas y baño, además del correspondiente 'Sleeping Porch,' en donde cómodamente instalamos o más bien dicho, ya estaban instalados tres catres."[30] ("Our home was a toy, resembling a mission, recently completed. It had five bedrooms and a bath, in addition to the corresponding 'Sleeping Porch,' where we placed conveniently, or better said, three cots were already there.")

The style of Olga's home is a mixture of Spanish and American architecture, but it is apparent that her home in Mexico was much larger than her home in El Paso. Her home in Texas, however, has the traditional porch, which she noticed as she crossed the state. Now she has one of her own. Moreover, she will sleep on the porch, as Texans were accustomed to doing before the introduction of air conditioning. It is evident that Olga is experiencing cultural adaptation, the consequence of transculturalization.

Throughout the memoir, Olga has been cognizant of the *mexicano's* presence in the United States. She speaks of the Mexican nun on the ship, the Mexican man who married the German woman in Texas City, the Mexican woman who sat with her in the for-colored-only seats in the train (although this woman was of Mexican citizenship, it is evident by Olga's tone that she was an Indian of Mexico or, at least, of a lower socioeconomic status), and the displacement of black laborers in the agricultural fields outside Houston by Texas Mexicans; consequently, it is not surprising that in the last entry, Olga Beatriz Torres treats the Chicana as her subject matter.

As is customary for Mexicans of the upper class, once the family has settled in El Paso, they begin their search for an efficient maid, and when they do hire one, it is a Chicana. Olga states,

> Entre las mujeres que llegaron en busca de colocación, aceptamos a una que aseguró saber cuanto hubiera en materia de cocina; pero en realidad, poco sabía la pobre; pero en cambio, aprendí con ella el dialecto que hablan aquí la mayor parte de los mexicanos que ya tienen mucho tiempo en ésta.[31]
> [Among the numerous women who came to apply for the job, we accepted one that assured us that she knew everything there was to know about the kitchen, but, in reality, the poor thing knew very little. On the other hand, I learned from her the dialect that the majority of the Mexicans who have lived here for a long time speak.]

Olga's maid, a Chicana, becomes her mentor. It is through her that she learns the language of transculturalization. Olga observes that the Spanish language of the *mexicano* in Texas is not easily understood. She explains:

> Porque debes saber, tía Ciria, que no es tan fácil entender el castellano de los mexicanos de Texas, los cuales, en contacto con los americanos, han mexicanizado muchas palabras inglesas y han anglicanizado muchas castellanas, de manera que su dialecto, es una mezcla de español e inglés, incorrectos los dos, mal pronunciados los dos e incomprensibles en verdad.[32]
> [Because you must know, Tía Ciria, that it is not easy to understand the Castilian of the Texas Mexicans, who because of

A Transcultural Voyage

their contact with Americans have Mexicanized many English words and anglicized many Spanish words, to the extent that their dialect is a mixture of Spanish and English, both incorrect, both badly pronounced, and truly incomprehensible.]

Olga illustrates her point to her Tía Ciria by recording the excuse given by the maid for being late to work:

Venía yo de la Esmelda ayer; y pedí en el carro un trance para ir al Dipo, en donde me habían dicho que había una marqueta, y yo necesitaba comprar unas mechas, y ver si había un calentón barato, para el cual ya tengo bastante leña en la yardita; pero cuanto ya iba llegando, se descompuso el traque y tuve que esperar, dirigiéndose a la casa de la familia López, de Chihuahua. Allí los babis habían roto un paquete de espauda, de ese que se usa en los bisquetes; y me pidió la señora prestado un daime, para comprar otro, y como yo no tenía más que ese, tuve que hacer el viaje a pie, y me puse mala, por eso no vine temprano.[33]

[Yesterday, I was coming from the Esmelda and I asked in the carro for a trance to go to the dipo where I had been told there was a marqueta, and I needed to buy some mechas and see if there was an inexpensive heater, for which I had enough wood in the yardita, but when I was about to arrive, the traque broke and I had to wait, so I went to the home of the López family of Chihuahua. The babis had torn open a package of espauda, the kind that is used in bisquetes. The lady asked me to lend her a daime to buy another one and since I didn't have any other except that one, I had to walk and became sick, that's why I am late.]

Although this short explanation is for most Spanish speakers living in the border area of Texas very easily understood, it was originally difficult for Olga to decipher. However, by the end of her memoirs, Olga becomes a translator of the language of the border people, in essence, a translator of border culture. In fact, she learns the language and translates and transports it back to Mexico. She writes,

¿Entendiste? Verdad que no? Pues allá va la explicación: *esmelda*, le llaman aquí al barrio en donde está la fundición de metales que en inglés se llama **Smelter**. Carro le llaman al tranvía, porque en inglés se dice **car**. *Dipo*, es incorrección de *depot*, que en inglés es estación del ferrocarril. *Trance* es un boleto que dan en los tranvías para trasbordarse a otro tranvía sin pagar, del cual ya te hablé en otra carta, cuyo boleto en inglés se dice **tranfer**.[34]

[Did you understand? You didn't, did you? Well here goes the explanation: *esmelda* is what around here they call the neighborhood where the **Smelter** is located. *Carro* is what they call the *tranvía* because in English it is called **car**. *Dipo* is an incorrection of **Depot,** which means train station. *Trance* is a ticket that one receives in the trolley to **transfer** to another trolley without having to pay. I have already mentioned this act in a previous letter, such a ticket in English is called **transfer.**]

In addition to the translation, Olga gives the English origin of the anglicisms: "Marqueta dicen en vez de mercado, que en inglés es **market;** *mechas*, son cerillos, y lo han tomado del inglés *matches*, que significa cerillos."[35] ("They use the word *marqueta* rather than *mercado*, which in English means **market;** *mechas* are **matches,** and it has been taken from the English word, **matches.]**

Olga identifies other Castilian barbarisms, such as *calentón*, and the Mexicanization of English words such as *yardita*, *bisquetes*, and *daime*, and continues her last entry by stating, "Ya con estas explicaciones podrás traducir el incomprensible castellano de Carlota.[36] ("Now with these explanations, you should be able to translate the incomprehensible Spanish of Carlota.")

Olga Beatriz Torres concludes her text by declaring, "¡Americanos y compatriotas, necesitan intérprete para entenderles."[37] ("Americans and compatriots need interpreters to understand them.")

Olga's last entry illustrates her total control of the three Texas border-area languages—Spanish, English, and the dialect of the *mexicano* in the United States—which Bruce-Novoa classifies as interlingualism.[38] It is evident that Olga's transculturalization is complete, a completeness that is apparent in her control of the three linguistic fields that surround individuals living in the Southwest. Where two distinct languages come together, the inevitable occurs; the emergence of the third linguistic medium of communication, an interlingual medium, is to be expected. Consequently, as much as the members of El México de Afuera insisted they would maintain their Mexican culture intact and their Spanish language pure, Torres's memoirs demonstrate that as soon as one culture comes in contact with another, a third culture is inevitable, a phenomenon that serves to enrich both mother cultures, if they do not insist on the naive ideology that a culture can be monolithic. Thus although Olga Beatriz Torres's text is a product of the Generation of El México de Afuera, it is also a Chicana text, and an American literary text.

✝ NOTES ✝

Footnote information is based on the original text, *Memorias de me viaje* (El Paso: La Patria del Norte, 1918).

1. See the following text: Mario T. García, *Desert Immigrants: The Mexicans of El Paso, 1880–1920* (New Haven: Yale University Press, 1981); Mario T. García, *Mexican Americans: Leadership, Ideology, and Identity, 1930–1960* (New Haven: Yale University Press, 1989); Richard A. García, *Rise of the Mexican American Middle Class: San Antonio, 1929–1941* (College Station: Texas A&M University Press, 1991); Guadalupe San Miguel, Jr., *"LET ALL OF THEM TAKE HEED": Mexican Americans and the Campaign for Educational Equality in Texas, 1910–1981* (Austin: University of Texas Press, 1987).

2. Querido Moheno, "En el Vigesimo Aniversario de *La Prensa*," *La Prensa* of San Antonio, Texas, 13 February 1933, p. 3.

3. Féderico Allen Hinojosa, *El México de Afuera y su reintegración a la patria* (San Antonio: Artes Gráficas, 1940): 8.

4. Ibid., 5–10.

5. Ibid.

6. Ibid., 51–71.

7. Luis Leal, "The Spanish-Language Press: Function and Use," *Americas Review* 17, no. 3–4 (Fall–Winter): 157–62.

8. Dennis J. Perle, "The Novels of the Mexican-Revolution Published by the *Casa Editorial Lozano*," *Americas Review* 17, no. 3–4 (Fall–Winter): 163–68.

9. Juan Bruce-Novoa, *Martín Luis Guzmán, La Sombra del Caudillo: Version periódistica* (Mexico: Universidad Nacional Autónoma de México, 1987).

10. Stanley L. Robe, *Azuela and The Mexican Underdogs* (Berkeley and Los Angeles: University of California, 1979), 83–92.

11. Ibid., 83–84.

12. Ibid. `

13. "Veinte Años de Vida," *La Prensa* of San Antonio, Texas, 13 February 1993, p. 3.

14. "Los Sentirse de Este México," *La Prensa* of San Antonio, Texas, 1 August 1933, p. 3.

15. Ibid.

16. Ibid.

17. Olga Beatriz Torres, *Memorias de mi viaje* (El Paso: El Paso del Norte, 1918).

18. Ibid., 11.

19. To maintain authenticity, words that appeared in English in the Spanish version have been boldfaced in the English translation.

20. Ibid., 18.

21. Ibid., 25.

22. Ibid., 35–36.

23. Ibid., 40.

24. Ibid., 47.

25. Ibid., 57.

26. Ibid., 75.

27. Ibid., 79–80.

28. Ibid., 90–91.

29. Ibid., 101.

30. Ibid.

31. Ibid., 102.

32. Ibid.

33. Ibid., 103.

34. Ibid.

35. Ibid., 103–4.

36. Ibid., 104.

37. Ibid.

38. Juan Bruce-Novoa, "Spanish-Language Loyalty and Literature," in *Retrospace: Collected Essays on Chicano Literature* by Juan Bruce-Novoa (Houston: Arte Público Press, 1990): 41–51.

✤ To the Reader: ✤

This collection of letters, in which Olga—a child of 13 years—recounts impressions of her trip, does not pretend to have literary merit.

We plead with critics to read with indulgence her first work, compiled by us as an homage to her literary precocity so that her memories would have a longer life span than we would be able to provide in the newspaper pages of "El Paso del Norte," where they were originally printed.

—The Editors
[Torres's dedication]

To Mr. Silvestre Terrazas
Editor of "La Patria"
Respectfully
Olga Beatriz
El Paso, January 17, 1919

✠ A LOS LECTORES: ✠

Esta colección de cartas, en que Olga—niña de 13 años de edad— cuenta las impresiones de su viaje; no tienen pretensiones literarias de ninguna clase.

Rogamos a los críticos vean con indulgencia este su primer trabajo, coleccionado por nosotros, como un homenaje a su precocidad literaria y para que tengan sus "Memorias" vida más larga que la que les podríamos dar en las columnas periodísticas de "El Paso del Norte," en donde originalmente las publicamos.

—Los Editores
[Torres dedication, Spanish]

Al Sr. Don Silvestre Terrazas
Director de "La Patria."
Respetuosamente.
Olga Beatriz
El Paso, Enero 17, 1919.

✝ Exodus ✝

Tía Ciria,

The sun was rising in Mixcoac. It was four-thirty and with a sense of urgency created by the excitement of an approaching trip, I ate breakfast quickly. We left—a train from San Angel stopped at the Candelaria Train Station. We boarded immediately and I saw "Villa Olga," my beloved home, lost amidst the density of the trees.

Twenty minutes later, we arrived in Mexico City: on San Juan de Letrán Street, from there an automobile took us to the Buena Vista Station. Mexico City appeared livelier than usual. It had been a long time since I had seen the city this early in the day: closed stores, slow moving carriages, yawning guards, a small dog passed by . . .

Cordero waited for us at the station. Remember him? Papá's secretary. We boarded the Pullman. I was speechless. Joy? Sadness? Maybe both. We were delayed for a long time, infinitely. Finally, the train started to move, slowly at first, then faster, in such a manner that telephone posts and houses appeared to gallop at full speed toward the city.

Train stations all identical: large, poorly constructed wooden sheds, others of stone, but always of the same architectural design— angular and unattractive.

We arrived at Esperanza, and we were off to eat "something other than Pullman's canned food," remarked my Papá. And we ate. The restaurant is managed by Chinese and it consists of a large room with tables parallel to each other around which passengers quickly sit and serve themselves. Since waiters lay out different types of food platters on the center of the tables, everyone helps himself. There were many appetizing foods, but I didn't taste any. They were eaten by those less courteous than I or by those hungrier than I. "All aboard," announced the conductor and walked away.

At eight P.M., we arrived at Soledad and the conductor informed us that this was the location where we were to sleep and we stayed there. During times of peace, and, on other trips, we slept in Veracruz, but war is unfortunate for all, even for myself beginning to live life.

The heat was unbearable, and since then—June 28—we noticed the heat in all parts of the country. We left the building and wandered throughout the village; in the street's darkness, we saw soldiers sleeping on sidewalks; others were chatting. "The town is a military camp," responded a woman I questioned.

The next day we were transferred to a military train where we checked in our luggage and my wrist watch was stolen. Remember, the one engraved with my initials? Then we were transported to Tejería, the front line of Huerta's soldiers.

We were informed that from Tejería to Tembladeras (the front line of American soldiers) we were to travel by foot, but tomorrow I'll let you know how we did because this letter is getting to be too long.

Your niece who loves you,

Olga Beatriz.

✛ On the Road ✛

Tía Ciria:

As I mentioned in my previous letter, we arrived in Tejería on a military train. There, moments before we got off the train, three suspicious looking individuals, cautiously observing all passengers, boarded the train. Holding out a telegram, one of them approached my father and spoke with him. Later, shaking his head, he moved away.

We got off. Here and there, an artillery lieutenant interrogated passengers. He asked if the convoy had been assaulted on its way to Tejería, if there was peace in Mexico City, and other things—in my opinion, he should have known these things better than we did.

Quickly, Papá loaded us on a covered carriage which charged a peso per person. There were more passengers than space.

Thus we continued to Tembladeras, a bumpy ride, since we were following the railroad tracks which were destroyed by the orders of General Maass when he escaped from Veracruz and which were covered with burnt brush.

The heat was like a furnace fire. The landscape was gorgeous. Though I had seen it several times before, it always seemed the same: trees everywhere, millions of flowers, plants all around.

The carriage stopped in front of a country store in the doorway of which a second lieutenant and four soldiers stood; they were the last of Huerta's soldiers we were to see. We got out of the carriage and continued our trip on foot because the carriage could not continue following the tracks since a freight car blocked it. The walk was long: more than one kilometer beneath a burning sun, over scorching land, skipping from tie to tie. Imagine, Aunt!

We waited for two hours; several men who had come from Veracruz sold lemonade for fifty centavos. It was mouth-watering.

As they sold their merchandise, they entertained customers with frightening accounts of the American takeover of Veracruz, of how the glass windowpanes of the buildings in the center of town were shattered by bullets, of how the people of Veracruz, upon learning of the army's withdrawal, came together in the streets and fired at those disembarking the American ship; however, because most of the people did not own firearms, they were satisfied to throw rocks at them. They spoke of battleships shooting grenades at buildings, especially at the marine school which was eventually destroyed; they recounted the incident with such frenzy thus producing a sensation of horror and hate against the assailants.

I was tempted to ask that we return to Mexico, but thoughts of father's political persecution, of the horrifying destruction of the charming city by Zapata's hordes, of the unjust vengeance in the hands of government partisans, of the assassination by unknown assassins of people who were thought to be against the government and, finally, hearing of the horror the war was spreading throughout the land made me realize that returning to the City of Palaces would be total stupidity.

Amidst these reflections which helped shorten the waiting period, I heard a whistle blow. A dense column of black smoke in the woods indicated the arrival of a train.

It arrived with individuals dressed in khaki and wearing wide-rim felt hats traveling in the front cow guard. Each one carried a rifle on his shoulder. "Who are they?" I asked.

"American soldiers," answered my father and emotionally added, "It is sad that tyranny has obliged me to seek sanctuary among these men."

We boarded the train and after having ridden for a long time, we saw a doctor (actually, I learned that he was a doctor) and a young man carrying a box of papers enter our car. What did they want? Some of the passengers told us that we were to be vaccinated. Can you believe that! We didn't like that at all, but what could we do? Without the vaccination, we would not be permitted off the train.

And it was something to see: men taking off their shirts and rolling up their sleeves to bare their arms; the same with women. We were all vaccinated by means of a few scratches made by a few thin wires and the injection of serum. We were asked our names and certificates were issued.

As we arrived at "Los Cocos," I saw American military camps on both sides of the tracks, strong, yellow army tents, and close to them were rooms made of wooden frames covered with chicken wire. Inside, American soldiers seated on long rectangular benches in front of narrow tables were eating. Here and there, a detachment was guarding the area.

At 12:30 P.M. the train arrived in Veracruz. Again, we checked in our luggage. There was shouting, here and there, and due to their ignorance of the language, mute American soldiers walked everywhere.

Twenty minutes later, we were in the hotel.

Your niece,

Olga Beatriz.

✛ Veracruz ✛

Tía Ciria:

In Veracruz, in addition to the misery caused by the heat, we had something worse: horrible food, and from what I have heard, the worse the food, the higher the price. The fish was tolerable, the meat was disgusting, the vegetables were homeopathic.

"Figure it out for yourself," the hotel maître d' told me, "with the arrival of the Americans and the lack of routes of communication, lettuce costs thirty *centavos*, peas can be found only in cans and for a *peso*, eggs cost one *real* . . ." and the list goes on and on. What he was saying was true.

Even ice was scarce to the point that it was necessary to bring a ship loaded exclusively with ice from Galveston. To think that the citizens of Veracruz needed to drink ice water all day long.

The city was a burning oven, so that I preferred to be beneath the shade of a tree or beneath the breeze of an electric fan in my bedroom rather than to go out into those scorching asphalt streets.

Furthermore, there was nothing else to see, except American soldiers with rifles on their shoulders guarding the streets in pairs, keeping step, their khaki jackets sweat-soaked as if they had purposely soaked them.

At other times, at least, there were buzzards eating trash off the streets, but today, because of the American military commander-in-chief's rigid restrictions on sanitary conditions, not one of those repulsive animals was seen anywhere.

One morning, I went to the sea baths: a thick fenced-in enclosure prevents sharks from entering a large section of the sea. One enters the swimming area through ramps placed on both sides and on the rear of the enclosure, perpendicular to the enclosure, was a building especially for the swimming club where refreshments were sold.

On both sides of the entrance were several small rooms where swimmers could change into their swimming suits . . . and jump into the water!

A swim is a pleasant thing anywhere, but in Veracruz these sea baths, especially, are a piece of liquid pleasure, and I had so much pleasure that I was on the verge of learning to swim.

In the bay and farther away from it, foreign ships of all sizes and shapes were keeping watch over the security of their nations. One afternoon, I counted forty-two war vessels. The major part of them were American battleships; from a distance, they seemed to be frozen on the surface of the sea like floating cathedrals—due to their enormous towers.

One afternoon I went to the naval school, and as I contemplated the windows broken by the battleship cannon balls, the windows seemed to me to make a horrible gesture of anger: less against the invaders and more for the citizens who with their excesses submit their nation to such trials and tribulations.

Early in the mornings and later in the afternoons, the streets of Veracruz and the municipal courtyard were filled with American soldiers and sailors and a few Spaniards, Frenchmen, and Englishmen who were ignominiously exploited by the vendors of curiosities who were permitted to sell their pieces of junk for an arm and a leg.

General Funston ordered that chairs be placed in front of the lighthouse which had been converted into American military quarters and which was on the edge of the sea, so that the people who lived on the harbor could relax watching talking movies as they sunbathed in the beach from early in the afternoon to ten in the evening.

Letters (English)

The movies could also be seen by American soldiers lying on the beach. The bad thing, Aunt, was the music—the military music which destroyed the eardrum with its monorhythmic pieces—If Mr. Cerbón, (give him my greetings) my piano professor, had only heard them . . .!

Meanwhile, the days went by and a ship to take us out of Veracruz was still unavailable: all the ships that arrived and left were battleships. Finally, the arrival of the **"City of Mexico"** was announced, and we rushed to get out of Veracruz.

The day it docked, we went to see it. How ugly, Aunt, but it was the only ship available and it was necessary to leave that aforementioned oven that was suffocating us!

Your niece,

Olga Beatriz.

✛ THE SEA ✛

Dear Tía:

Proud to have been born in the capital of the Republic, I wish that everything that carries its name would be as big and as beautiful as it is, but the ship "**City of Mexico**," is a piece of junk that dishonors the name.

I am not familiar with many ships, but the ones I have seen in Veracruz when we have been in port, such as the "**Champagne**," the "**Morro Castle**," and others are a hundred times superior.

Someone said, and maybe he is right, that the "**City of Mexico**" is exclusively a cargo ship and that explains why its cabins, which are not even twenty, are like jail cells where one suffers the unspeakable.

I will describe the ship: in the center, beneath the deck is the dining area, a rectangular space of about six by ten meters, with two narrow and parallel tables; in the back of the room, you will find a piano, horribly out of tune and old.

Some cabin doors open into the dining room, which makes me believe that the dining area used to be a **hall.** Of course, if one is having breakfast and a door to one of the cabins opens, one can see the latecomers getting dressed or the seasick ones sleeping semi-naked.

We had cabin number 5, one of the better ones because it was located in the hallway that crossed the ship from side to side and it had two skylight windows that faced the sea. At least, the cool breeze came in through there!

On the deck were the commander's quarters, now divided into two sections. He occupied half of it, and the Newman family rented the other half at a high price. Over this section was another compartment where the wireless telegraph office was located.

On opposing ends were what is called the prow and stern and in the lower part, machinery, cranes, cables, gears, etc., and the entrance to the holding room which took up most of the belly of the ship.

On June 3 at 3:00 P.M., the day assigned as the departing day, we found ourselves in this floating prison. The deck was filled with people who were looking out from lounge chairs which my father had bought in the harbor and which were made from some painted yellow poles and pieces of old canvas.

I didn't know whether all these people were going to travel, but they were too many for the ship. It was five o'clock, and we remained anchored while cranes continued loading bundles and placing them in the holding room, without stopping . . . five-thirty and the same . . . six o'clock and the same thing . . . finally, at six-fifteen, I heard a strange noise. I looked to both sides of the ship, and I saw water spouting out of several holes. "The propeller is starting to work," a neighbor told me politely.

Like a charm, those who were not passengers quickly began to disembark, and very soon there were only a few of us on the deck. The body of the ship started to move away from the pier and turn around because the prow was pointing toward the port, and now with the ship en route toward the sea, it began to move away from the city.

Suddenly passengers started shouting and gathering at one end of the ship and the ship stopped alongside a Spanish cruiser, "*Carlos V*." I went to look; it was a delayed passenger on a small motorboat arriving at full speed . . . a ladder was thrown out and he climbed on board.

We continued to move away and arrived at the estuary, that's the name given to where the bay ends and the open sea begins. Then there were new shouts, again people began to gather, and I saw an-

other motorboat, another delayed passenger who had missed the ship
. . . the ship stopped, the ladder was thrown out, and, with some diffi-
culty, a woman and her luggage, a large trunk and two suitcases, were
brought on board. The man from the small boat started to scream that
he had not been paid. She had given him only ten *pesos*, he asked for
five more, and we had to give it to him before we could leave!

Meanwhile on the beach, hundreds of small handkerchiefs bid
us farewell; we responded from the ship . . . I too waved my handkerchief and cried as I thought of you, Aunt, staying behind to suffer the
horrors of war.

We passed close to the battleships whose sailors also bid us farewell. Little by little, the city, towers, and the beach disappeared; quickly,
I saw the interminable water underneath . . . and an endless sky above.

Never had I seen such a thing: many times in my readings I have
read descriptions of the sea, more or less detailed, more or less beautiful, but the truth is that no one who has, at least, a small fraction of
soul in his body can stop admiring this enormous beauty.

As for me, I must say that I felt admiration and fear:
admiration because the landscape is grandiose and beautiful—the sunlight as it broke over the waves produced an arabesque of different
colors so varied so those who speak of the "blue sea," of the "green
sea" are mistaken. The sunlight projects so many colors on the moving surface of the sea that it is neither green nor blue; it is an infinite
variety of colors. It is an admirable polychrome. I feared the sea too
because our ship felt like a light feather over the moving waves of the
ocean. From a distance, we could see large mountains of foamy water
that it appeared that they might bury our ship, and when we got close,
our light-feather ship surfaced over that roaring wave to wait on the
other side for another avalanche . . . and we continued in this manner—endlessly.

I abandoned my seat on the deck (a long canvas chair rustically made) and approached the rail to entertain myself by watching wave after wave go by as in an insane race, as one tried to catch up with the next, but never succeeding, and in the weaving of the waters, like in a foggy burlap, I could see fish of different sizes and colors playing and following the ship, unconcerned with the harsh disturbance on the water surface.

Suddenly, I began to feel a horrible uneasiness—I got a headache . . . I felt nauseated . . . my vision became blurry—the sea began to get larger and larger by the minute, and I went into a horrible full-blown suffering. I have never felt anything worse . . . Dad picked me up, took me down the climbing ladder, and laid me down in the cabin.

A little later, I noticed that my mother had joined me and that my father was fanning us. To Tarsela who wanted to know what was wrong with us, he answered,

"Seasickness, Tatitos, seasickness . . ."

Until my next letter.

Olga Beatriz.

✠ FAMILY ON BOARD ✠

Tía Ciria:

For two days, I was trapped in the cabin with my mother, both horribly seasick . . . on the second day, my seasickness increased with frightening anguish. Can you imagine that by two small windows of the cabin, the ones through which I felt the wind on my face, I began to see the sky turn black? Huge bolts of lightning which seemed to set everything on fire were followed by thunder louder than the canons we heard in the war games of Tlacopac.

Then it started to rain abundantly, and the sea moved in such a manner that it seemed to take hold of the ship. The ship creaked, doors opened and closed, like the houses of Mexico during the earthquake of June 7, 1911. Do you remember? Mother and I didn't know what to do. Fortunately, one of the waiters who had waited on us passed by the Columbus corridor, and I asked him to call my father.

Meanwhile, a thick fog surrounded us, and at every minute, a high-pitched whistle blew, increasing my fear as it announced the danger of collision to other ships that might be near.

A sailor, a horrible and fierce giant who carried a few objects that appeared like fragments of a cushioned board, quickly entered our cabin and told us something in his language as he placed four of the boards underneath the lower beds.

Later, I learned that they were lifesavers, in case of a shipwreck!

Behind him, my Papá arrived, accompanied by a Japanese sailor, Denza Mori. When he saw our fear and Papá translated the cause of it, he calmed us by telling us that it was nothing and that it would last only an hour . . . and Denza Mori was right. An hour later, the sky was again beautifully blue.

On the third day, we were cured of the seasickness and I went to the deck, now without fear. I could eat something and at seven in the evening, the dinner hour, I went to the dining room, and I got to know all the passengers. I learned that all of them had become seasick, but most of them were now fine and laughed as they spoke of their seasickness.

That night, I saw a splendid thing: the rising of the moon over the immensity of the sea. The moon was enormous. It seemed that all the waves became a moving silver. It looked as if the moon was spurting "frost" of the kind that is abundant on the manger on New Year's Eve. It was so beautiful that I can not describe it, but you can imagine it!

All the passengers had learned to trust one another, all seemed to create a single family. We were people who had not known one another before and who probably would not see one another ever again, but in the meantime, we trusted each other so that we all seemed to be related, or, at least, very close friends.

To entertain you a little, I will describe the passengers. Imagine two St. Teresa nuns, an older Catalonian and an American, but of Mexican parents; they were going to San Antonio, Texas, as professors of a Catholic school. The girl was also going to see her parents whom she had not seen in four years since she had lived at St. Teresa College in Mixcoac. Do you remember it?

A tall, strong man, Rafael Elorduy, a rich landowner, relative of the great musician Ernesto Elorduy and author of the "Vals Capricho" that I play and that you like so much.

This passenger distinguished himself because since the day he boarded the ship until he disembarked in Texas City, he was gravely seasick, remained reclined on a lounge chair over a blanket, day and night. I spoke with him several times and he told me that he had properties in Zacatecas, but that he did not know what had happened to them—happenings of war! He was accompanied by an employee, a young Spaniard, happy and talkative, who brought him "*Apolinaris*" all day long; it was the only thing his stomach could take.

There was also a young man, Salinas, with his wife and a young child the age of Rojana, my sister, who often played with her. There was a cavalry captain and another tall, dark man who were going to Sonora to reunite themselves with revolutionaries. Mrs. Mavoy, a dark Mexican with two children who cried day and night, was going to Galveston to look for her husband. This woman came from Mexico in the same Pullman as ours. Do you remember the woman who was sitting next to our seat when we said goodbye?

Also traveling were two Redo men from Sinaloa, one with his son and the other, happy and talkative, with a strong voice who enjoyed alarming the two nuns with religious questions. There was an English woman with a young girl; they were going to take a ship to England from Galveston. She told me her name, but I forgot it.

Also the Japanese Captain, Denza Mori, the same one I spoke of at the beginning of this letter, second commander of Itzumo.

On board was the Newman family who was going to Torreón, two French women, and three Americans. Toward the end, almost when the trip was over, I met a school classmate of my mother, Mrs. Clementina Arteaga from Aguascalientes, who was going with a young girl and four nieces to Houston to meet her husband, the lawyer Calderón. The poor woman had four days of miserable seasickness.

Finally, on July 7, the ship docked in Galveston, and after a long wait, the health inspector arrived, introduced himself to the Captain in his bedroom, spoke with him for almost an hour, and then left. Later, we learned that he denied permission to disembark, that the whole ship was to be fumigated, and that he would not examine the passengers until the following day. Imagine our anguish to see the port and to be condemned to a day of imprisonment!

Olga Beatriz.

✠ Port of Call ✠

Tía Ciria:

When we learned of the health inspector's decision, everyone protested. There were some who ridiculed the order and took a rowboat to the beach, but those who knew of the incident, those who had traveled at other times said, "If you get off the ship, you will see that in addition to going to jail for a couple of days, paying a fine, and suffering other abuse, they will send you back to Veracruz, if not in this ship, in another."

In the face of this threat, the protest was quieted; those who had been eager to violate the law began to conform. With dejection and laughter, they took their folding chairs to get away from the heat and began to read or chat, facing Galveston which seemed to boil near the sea.

Then I learned that it was indispensable that the health inspector examine each passenger, since entry into the United States is not permitted to anyone carrying a contagious disease.

Furthermore, I became aware that we were to be examined by an immigration inspector, for neither is one permitted to disembark if one does not have a certain amount of money, no less than fifty *pesos*. One must be, in addition, an honorable and hard-working person and of good breeding.

Here the poor are considered as dangerous as those with a contagious disease.

I was contemplating all of this when I saw a white shadow come out of the telegraph office and jump into the sea—followed by another, and then another . . . we ran to see; they were three passengers who jumped from that height to swim in the sea; I felt like following them; it was so hot.

The current was so strong that one of the passengers almost was unable to grab the cable that was thrown to him.

The telegrapher, a skinny one whose face was rarely seen, having nothing to do since we reached port, was tempted by the view of the swimmers, and . . . splashed into the water from an enormous height, swam three strokes, and hit the side of the ship. That morning we entertained ourselves with these actions, and then we were off to suffer the horrors of the awful food. How horrible one eats in this ship. My God!

After eating, the passengers' protest resumed because we were condemned to the demands of the health inspector as we were forced to spend the day in sight of the port, but then I learned the motive.

Before arriving in Veracruz, the ship, **City of Mexico,** had spent a day in the port of Coatzacoalcos and we were assured that two cases of yellow fever had been reported there. Even though no passengers came from there, if the seamen had disembarked, it would be necessary to wait six days from the day they had disembarked: one from Coatzacoalcos to Veracruz, four that the trip took, and one waiting. Total, six!

Soon a strong odor of sulphur started to seep through all the windows and stairways; we all started to cough and choked. There wasn't a place where we could be that we didn't feel the symptoms of asphyxia. The ship was being disinfected, and so were we.

Until almost ten o'clock at night, we could not enter the cabin because of the sulphur odor that lingered in the room. In the meantime, with the moon that seemed to smile from the sky and laugh at our change of fortune, I sent forth to you a greeting. Did you receive it?

The next day at midday, the ship headed toward Texas City, but the previous afternoon, I had seen the first thing that caught my attention in the United States. The train arrived at the edge of the beach and pieces of the dock where it had stopped began to move away from the coast. Pretty soon it went by us and I could see the passenger train float with the passengers seated serenely as if they were traveling by land, but the locomotive and the cars stood over a section of the rails that was being towed on a big plank or floating dock which was pulled by a tugboat that was at its side. It went by us and continued to the opposite beach. It docked, and the locomotive began to move as if it were moving on solid land.

In Texas City, the doctor examined us, one by one, especially the eyes; he separated two passengers that looked suspicious to him. Then the immigration inspector asked us where we were coming from, where we were going and how much money we were carrying.

Then he inspected the luggage with a new procedure that seemed to take forever, and at five in the afternoon, we finally stepped on American soil. It was about time!

Olga Beatriz.

✠ Texas City ✠

My Dear Aunt:

The first thing I thought as I got off the train and saw my surroundings was the following: "And this is American soil? This is the United States?"

In front of me, to the right and to the left, extended a large, two-story, wooden warehouse with an endless series of numbered doors, badly constructed and an ugly sight.

The roughly constructed wooden dock could be seen through the planks that formed the floor, a scaffolding made of enormously thick beams that were sunken in a greenish and murky water.

Inside the gigantic warehouse (to this date, I have not seen anything bigger than this) were piles of bundles, boxes, bags, etc., and I knew that each one of these piles made up the complete cargo of a ship. Here the cargo occupied only a small portion of the warehouse.

Alongside the walls were fire extinguishers and some other apparatus which was connected to telephone lines. One need only press a button to announce a fire to the fire station.

Behind and around the warehouse, except on the side facing the sea, were large sections of land, ugly and nitrous, non-arable lands, similar to the ones that are seen in Nonoalco, Mexico, or in Nativitas or San Andrés Tetepilco. They were so alike that the same tall fodder grass that grows there also grows here.

The sea was another thing with ships of all sizes and with distinct names: some in English, others in French, a few in German, many small ones in Spanish. Negro painters were painting the sides of all the ships from the waterline to the deck, standing on boards held on by cables and balanced on the surface of the sea, quite calm for sure.

My father arranged for the transfer of the luggage to the railroad station that was to take us to Houston because Mother snubbed Texas City; "This place must not even have hotels," she said, and I agreed with her.

Beneath a scorching sun, we started to walk toward the warehouse, while the rest of the passengers continued to walk the length of the dock.

We finally arrived at the warehouse and followed an ugly and dusty path; I won't say street because I consider a street to be a space more or less wide enough to function as a traffic conductor and permit access to houses, and there weren't any homes here.

We arrived at the first one, in front of the electric train station, and my disillusionment was great. Imagine a wooden shack with interior divisions which make it into a home and store at the same time. The doors were covered with screens to keep the flies and mosquitos out. Outside, it had a little dirty wooden bench used by passengers waiting for the train, and that shack, the "property" of a Mexican married to a German woman, was the only building in sight.

I could not restrain myself and asked, "Is this the United States?"

And then I learned that this was an emerging town, that four years ago there was nothing in this place, that it was a suburb, the outskirts of Galveston, but a company constructed some docks and warehouses here and made it known that this place was a place with a great future, that it was a better location than New Orleans or Galveston to ship out merchandise destined for Panama from the United States.

"So you see, child, this very recent town, these lands so ugly for you, will be within a short period of time a big city," expressed the Mexican owner of the store. "Three years ago when I built this building, there were only one hundred persons; now there are eight thousand people, without counting the fact that there are thousands of soldiers who are waiting to be shipped to Mexico from one moment to the next," he added.

The train was late and we took an automobile to sightsee. And then I realized the Mexican was right.

Asphalt streets, sprinkled with rows of houses on both sides of the street, clothing stores, bars, hotels of three and four stories, movie houses filled with people, drugstores, restaurants, cafés, and musicians could be seen. It was truly an emerging town, a town that would very soon be a big, big city.

People of all classes were on the streets, but American soldiers predominated among individuals who entered and exited all the buildings, gathering particularly within bar and theater doorways.

Suddenly, the sound of thunder made me raise my eyes to the sky. The sky suddenly darkened. The thunder was followed by another and then a tremendous storm broke.

We took refuge in a café, in front of the plaza. By the time people crossed the street and reached the sidewalk, they were dripping wet . . . suddenly we saw an avalanche of water in the theater . . . we could see its entrance from our table.

People came out running and laughing, soaked to their knees. They appeared pleased.

At ten o'clock in the evening, we were able to leave. It had stopped raining.

Olga Beatriz.

✠ Movement Inland ✠

Fifteen minutes later, we boarded the train en route to Texas Junction, where we were to transfer to a streetcar that would take us to Houston.

The night was extremely dark; consequently, I did not pay attention to the road, but due to a trip I took a couple of days later from Houston to Texas City, I saw that there wasn't anything special in it: uncultivated land, non-arable land, and camps of American soldiers with army tents similar to the ones I described near Veracruz, and, finally, some large petroleum deposits of the **Water Pierce Company** were on the middle of the road.

Twenty minutes later, we were at Texas Junction.

I thought it was a small town, but I came to find out that it was a small train station that appeared deserted since there were no employees nor anything that made any movement.

An announcement that my father translated illustrated the way to stop the train or streetcar en route to Houston or to Galveston—the electrical route goes from one town to another. The procedure could not have been any easier nor more familiar to me: by day, one was to wave a handkerchief so that the engineer would see it, and by night, one was to light a match stick or any other light.

Very soon we noticed in the distance a beam of light projected by the searchlight of the train that bathed the countryside and made it appear as if the railroad tracks were two parallel fires. We signaled and the train stopped.

This was a fairly large car. It was divided into thirds by a crystal folding screen door located in the third section where passengers who wished to smoke sat. The other two sections were for non-smokers and ladies.

The cars are elegant; the seats are covered with new red plush velvet and the metal part is yellow bronze, polished and brilliant. In regard to the layout, the seats are similar to the ones in the electric trolleys in Mexico City. But the electric buttons—with which the passengers can stop the vehicle without troubling themselves to pull the cord like in Mexico—are located in the side columns; one touches the button to ring the bell which is located in the back platform near the conductor who pulls the cords to the engineer's bell. Only the conductor can pull the cords since passengers are definitely prohibited from doing so.

In the rear platform of the street car are two doors, one on each side. One is an entrance and the other is an exit. As the train begins to move, both doors close immediately. Furthermore, the step folds up automatically so that one can not take the train while it is moving because of the lack of support and an entranceway.

As one enters the car, one pays or turns in the ticket; we bought ours in Texas City.

As I entered the car, I saw the car was almost full. My mother and Tatos walked ahead of me; Papá and one of the passengers from Veracruz sat down on one of the side seats, and the Mexican woman whom I met in the ship sat down with me on the last seat, to the left of the car, happy to have found an empty seat.

Our joy lasted for a short period. Five minutes later, the conductor approached me and started saying I don't know what in English as he pointed to a sign hanging over the seat; the words **"For Colored"** were printed on the board.

The conductor continued speaking in English, pointing to the sign. I answered in Spanish, "I don't understand." He insisted. I called my Papá and learned what he was saying.

I had to get up from the seat because it was reserved exclusively for Negroes since they are prohibited from sitting in the other sections of the train. These seats are held for them.

In a nearby station, a Negro couple boarded the train and contentedly sat down on my former seat. "**Oguita,**" horrified with the black couple, Tatos said, "Those apes, so **black,** took your seat?"

At eleven-thirty, we arrived in Houston.

Your niece,

Olga.

✠ HOUSTON ✠

Dear Tía:

We got off the electric train at Houston's **"Main Street,"** and found ourselves at the foot of a building: the **Rice Hotel,** extremely tall building. It was so tall that although the street was well lit, the highest part of it lost itself in the shadows of the night. When I could see the building by day, I saw that it had seventeen floors.

All around, on all four sides, other buildings were under construction, not as tall as the **Rice Hotel,** but still of eight, ten, and twelve floors; consequently, my first impression was that I was in an enormous tomb, whose four walls were lost in space.

We registered at the Bristol Hotel. The climate was unbearably hot, so much so that I opened the windows of my room and turned on the electric fan. In passing, I will tell you that the windows of the American buildings generally do not have those wooden panes that in Mexico are called shades, nor do they open to the sides like in Mexico. They only have glass panes placed in the following manner: the upper half of the window is fixed, while the lower half is pulled upward on top of the first, and that is how the window is opened, but not completely because the outer section is covered with a wire screen that keeps insects out.

The following morning, after breakfast, we took an automobile tour. They charged three dollars an hour.

Like watching a moving-picture screen, I began to see the city pass by as I listened to the explanations that the chauffeur gave and that my Papá translated. We stopped in some sections of town and entered the buildings. In this way, I was able to see the National Bank of South Texas, a building whose facade consisted of four gigantic columns on which rested an enormous marble triangle the width of the whole facade.

The Carter, an office building, is a large mass of sixteen floors with more than six hundred offices. The building of del Primer Banco Nacional (**First National Bank**), whose floors are made of marble just like its interior, is truly elegant. The Post Office building is a structure that occupies, with the garden that surrounds it, one block, but it is not as nice, beautiful nor as elegant as our General Post Office in Mexico.

I will tell you this: almost all the buildings are made of monotonous architecture. They are gigantic square masses sprinkled with rectangular windows that make me think of gigantic pigeon houses, without art or beauty of any kind . . . I assure you that my "Villa Olga" is a hundred times superior in beauty and elegance than these pigeon houses which have nothing worthy of admiration, except their size. Beyond the commercial center and along **Main Street** begin the homes of the rich, many of which are truly beautiful and very luxurious.

Between the asphalt streets and the sidewalks are English grass meadows, an endless grove that provides shade to pedestrians and gives the whole street a sense of beauty.

The houses are surrounded by plants and grass, and since yards are not divided, each block is an enchanting garden. You can visualize it better if you know that here it is not customary to have one house touch the other, side by side like in Mexico, so that each one is an isolated building and the garden in the front yard extends into the space between the buildings.

"A multimillionaire from New York lives here," mentioned the chauffeur as he pointed to a grand marble palace that occupied half a block—surrounded by one of the most beautiful gardens that I have seen—"but he comes to live here only one or two months during the winter; the rest of the year, the servants are the only ones that live here."

In this manner, stopping here and there along "**Main Street,**" we came out onto a big street, at the end of which we found Rice Institute. This deserves a separate letter.

Your niece,

Olga.

✣ Rice Institute ✣

Tía Ciria:

During our last letter, we were at the entrance of Rice Institute. This is a college of several gigantic buildings, built here and there, over an immense piece of land designated for the college: some of the buildings are completed while others will be completed very soon, since hundreds of men are working on their construction.

The Rice Institute will be a college where students of both sexes (since there will be a dormitory for women) will be able to study whatever they wish from elementary to professional school. One can study law, medicine, engineering, and liberal arts; everything is absolutely free, since Mr. Rice besides spending ten million American dollars or forty million Mexican *pesos* at today's rate of exchange has designated for the maintenance of said institute an amount equal to that.

We were informed that Mr. Rice proposed that the best American teachers teach the courses, so that this institute will be in a short period, I believe, one of the best universities of the United States.

We were told the story of this unusual altruism: Mr. Rice, a resident of New York came to Houston in search of health, which he soon found, and he also found something else, an intelligent American woman whom he married soon after. Later, he invested part of his capital in real estate around Houston, which he diversified and which yielded him some hundreds of thousands of dollars. Having found health, happiness, and wealth in Houston, he chose to repay the city with his gifts.

That's the way it was told to me and it is the way I tell you, but the fact is that Rice Institute is one of the most notable things in Houston, one of the things which caught my attention.

Toward the end of the afternoon, we left this colossal center of education and very rapidly went to the Colonial Park. It is very similar to the Luna Park in Mexico City; it has a significant collection of live animals, among them a variety of alligators, from a decimeter to four meters in size. Their scaly skin and huge mouths made us tremble with fear.

I also saw some seals of a meter and a half in length, whose black and oily bodies floated and sank in a thousand curves inside a tank the size of a room.

In some compartments were some ostriches, prettier than the ones in Chapultepec because they flaunted their entire plumage. There was also a collection of horrible snakes, several bears, monkeys, two tigers, and a Mexican parrot, according to the guard standing by the cage. This parrot fawningly bid us farewell saying, "**Goodbye.**"

It was beginning to get dark when we arrived at the **City Park,** which is one of the most picturesque parks of Houston, because of its irregular shape and its artificial stream which has small, rustic bridges built here and there and which are surrounded by green grass.

The park is large and it has several artistic diners around the patio, also rustically built, where American men and women eat, with great eagerness, large slices of watermelons, succulent and tasty, which were diligently sold to them by a Mexican whose countryside stand had printed on a cloth, "**Watermelons Five Cents a Slice**" (*sandía a cinco centavos rebanada*).

A group of small kids played on the grass, without fearing the police; here in these gardens children play on the grass while adults sleep beneath the trees, and no one bothers them. "That's what public parks are made for," the chauffeur told us.

As the night fell, we arrived at the hotel, crossing **"Main Street"** again which is the San Francisco Avenue of this American city, extravagantly lighted by candelabrums like the ones in that public street in my beloved Mexico!

Olga Beatriz.

✣ Bound for the Sea ✣

Dear Tía Ciria:

One morning . . . July 11 . . . the day began with an unbearable heat, to such a degree that the furniture, the walls, the floor, all seemed to be on the verge of catching on fire; they all felt hot. A passenger who arrived from Galveston told us that in that port the heat was tolerable and we decided to go to Galveston.

One can travel to this port by railroad or by electric train, without forgetting to consider that the trip can also be made by automobile because, in spite of the distance, there are magnificent highways. We opted for the electric train.

The electric train can be boarded on the principal street of Houston. One of its buildings is the train station, which has a large lobby. In front of it is a double row of benches meant to accommodate passengers; the ticket counter is in the rear of the train station. Also in this station, like in the train, there are some benches designated with the famous sign, **"For Colored."**

A five minute wait and the electric train arrived, the one that makes trips toward Galveston every hour. I mentioned in one of my previous letters that these cars are very elegant, and I had the opportunity to prove it on this trip. We left Houston at full speed; these trains run faster than the ones in Thalpam, Mexico; consequently, we were devouring the miles (here the word kilometer is not used) in a gradual descent toward the coast. As we moved, I learned some historical facts about Galveston. I will relate to you the ones that stand out.

Letters (English)

Galveston received its name in honor of a viceroy from Mexico, the Count of Galvez, during whose epoch several Spanish explorers landed in this place, which is an island. Later, the famous pirate, Jean Lafitte, converted the island into military headquarters and brought here the fruit of all the robberies he committed on the Gulf coast. It is believed that he buried here all the gold that he was able to acquire when he attacked the Spanish galleys which transported precious metals from Veracruz to the Iberian Peninsula. This occurred in 1816.

When Texas declared itself independent from our country, a Colonel, Miguel B. Menard, bought from the Texas Republic, for a trifle, all the land that the city of Galveston occupies, an indication that during this epoch, 1836, the island was still deserted.

By the following year, Colonel Menard had populated the site so that it was necessary to construct a special kind of seaport, but in the meantime, Gail Borden built a customhouse. In 1838, Colonel Amosa Taylor built the first pier.

The Civil War began in the United States, and Galveston had its share of suffering because it was blocked by the federal fleet.

Later, on January 1, 1863, a battle ensued near Galveston, and in June 1865, the city was finally seized.

These are the most important historical facts about Galveston, a relatively young town, as you know.

The road from Houston to Galveston is surrounded by little towns more or less beautiful; the inhabitants of the majority of these towns are dedicated to working orchards and vegetable fields.

Very soon, the orchards began to disappear and they were replaced by sandy land that announced the nearness of the beach, and it didn't take long before we saw the Gulf.

Rapidly, the train continued to move over one of the most notable things I have seen, a road constructed of cement that connected the coast land with the island of Galveston: the road consisted of a series of connecting bridges that permitted the sea waves underneath to move toward the beach.

This causeway is more than two kilometers long and in the center, truly an astonishing thing, there is an iron drawbridge that extends itself over the sea to permit trains, automobiles, and pedestrians to get to the island. When a ship draws near, a single man inside a small, wooden tower moves a small lever and the drawbridge lifts up smoothly as if it were made of straw, and the entrance opens up for the large steamships. Only if one sees it, will he believe it! Such a wonder cost two million American dollars.

I was still in awe when the electrical train entered the city of Galveston. I will tell you about it tomorrow.

Your niece,

Olga Beatriz.

✝ GALVESTON ✝

Tía Ciria:

One enters Galveston by following a large garden where palm trees, exquisitely kept, predominate, bordered on both sides by elegant and rich homes, among them some truly beautiful ones. We got off at the electric train station which does not have anything notable, since it consists of a kind of large carriage house where the trains stop beneath its roof. To its left, you find the ticket office with the same type of ticket arrangement as the one in Houston.

I walked quickly toward a newspaper and postcard stand where I bought some postcards consisting of photographs of the principal sites of the city.

In passing, I will tell you what is the most practical way of getting to know American cities, and, in general, those of other places. Even in Mexican cities, it has produced good results. As soon as one arrives at a place, one should buy postcards of the city that one is visiting because with these postcards one can quickly get an idea of the most important or the most picturesque buildings of the city. At once, one takes a carriage or an automobile (only automobiles are available here), and one tells the coachman or the chauffeur, as the case may be, that one wishes to see what is reproduced on the postcards. In this manner one doesn't have to put up with bothersome and expensive tour guides. According to Papá, they are the terror of all travelers because they make agreements with other coachmen and chauffeurs to increase their fees and extend endlessly the tour of the city.

Following this system, we took an automobile which took us along **Market Street,** one of the main streets; we crossed a park (**City Park**) in which stands a monument in honor of the soldiers and sailors who fought for the Confederate States and who died during the Civil War. The monument consists of a large quadrangular granite stone on top of which stands another monument of the same material and in the shape of a cube, two meters long per side, on top of which stands a statue, coarsely wrought, of an American soldier with an American flag wrapped around his left arm and a roll of paper, rather than a weapon, in his right hand.

We left the park, crossed several other streets, and arrived at a big sea wall which is bounded by the sea. Undoubtedly, this is the most beautiful site in Galveston.

This sea wall is made of concrete, paved with small blocks that make up the road, perfectly compressed and connected to each other that they give the impression that they are made of wood, so perfectly leveled that the automobile slides without the slightest bump, as if it were moving on a sheet of butter.

On one side of the highway which measures five miles in distance and which cost a million and a half dollars, extends the city with its happy, little houses which around here are called "bungalows" and are decorated with plants and flowers. On the opposite side of the highway is the Gulf of Mexico whose final waves, converted into foam about fifty meters away from the highway, die out.

Here and there and parallel to the highway, bathhouses constructed of wood are built on stilts four meters above the water. Used for sea baths, one named **"The Breakers"** predominates. From a distance, it resembles the grandstand of the *Condesa's* race tracks.

One of the most used bath houses is the **"Surf Bathing."** When we passed by it, there were more than three hundred persons bathing;

this included men, women, and children who wore the most extravagant and exotic swimming suits made of the brightest colors.

The scene is exquisite. Imagine, Tía, swimmers holding on and being supported by cables against the thrust of the waves; others grabbed by those holding on as the waves push them to shore and are thrown down on the sand; still others are stretched out on the beach.

Here and there, groups of children suddenly disappear in the waves and then reappear dripping water when the waves break. And all around, there is endless cheer, laughter, and happiness.

Driving on, we left the swimming area behind. At the end of the long highway, we found a military camp with its typical yellow tents; farther on, hidden between artificial hills that covered the green pasture, were some enormous cannons ready to defend the city.

On our return to the city, we continued on a grassy road on whose shoulders were piles of sticks and the remains of tents in complete disarray, as if the sea had destroyed a big ranch house, and piled here and there the remainder of the house. I asked what it was. "The remainder of an encampment of soldiers who were sent to Veracruz," the driver told us, as he turned on the fan in the car.

Until the next letter.

Your niece,

Olga Beatriz.

✠ THE CITY ✠

Tía Ciria:

Through ugly streets, which had accumulated water from the last rains and which had begun to take a greenish appearance, we arrived at the Galveston pier, or rather, at the piers, since there are several and all following the same pattern as the one in Texas City; that is to say, they are long wooden roads, on which one side is the sea, and the other is an endless row of warehouses. Not Galveston nor Texas City, in spite of the fact that their sea traffic is greater, possesses a pier that compares to the latest one in Veracruz.

One thing for sure, there were merchant ships of all types and from all over the world, as could be inferred by the variety of flags and their sailors. Close to the large ships, motorboats slithered in and out like small fish of countless colors; some, coarsely wrought, are meant to carry cargo; others, meant to be passenger boats, are beautifully finished, with a row of seats on each side and mounted above the deck.

On all sides there is such coming and going of people working that it made me dizzy; some are piling up merchandise near the doors of the warehouses; others are loading wheelbarrows and running with them to move the merchandise to different places. Cranes are lifting heavy bundles and loading them inside the ships; on the other side, train cars are loaded with merchandise, but with such quantity that they look like moving houses and vehicles. They had strong dual rubber wheels with a heavy chain wrapped around them that made a tremendous noise. Within this continuous movement were black, white, and brown men working together; it is impossible to walk in this area without the danger of being shoved or knocked down. Here, Aunt, everyone was moving around from one place to another, like my father, Julian, says when he gets mad, "Mind your own business! Mind your own business!"

By the time we left, dizzy with the movement of the workers, the light of the lighthouse named Bolívar, had been turned on, even though there was still daylight. The lighthouse is a cylindrical iron tower covered with tin sheets and painted in dull red and white, at the top the focus of a light bulb. The tower measures twenty-five to thirty meters in height and they assure us that the range of the lighthouse light is enormous.

Once we were in the city, we stopped for a moment in front of the Union Station. It is similar to the National Station in Mexico, except that this one is made of several floors. One thing caught my attention, a simple, iron stairway located in front of the building which connected all the floors, but it was terribly unsteady and dangerous for it to be the main staircase. I have seen this type of layout before in the buildings in Houston and Texas City, but it did not make the front of the building look as ugly as this one does here, and since I asked, I was told that since there are more frequent fires in the United States than in Mexico, the inhabitants of these "pigeon houses" need a fire escape.

We went by la Corte (**Court House**) which is the tribunal, a beautiful building that breaks the monotony of the rest of the buildings, and we continued through other streets until we again entered **Market Street** (*Calle del mercado*) where we got out of the automobile in front of an ice cream parlor. It cost us four and a half dollars to see the city of Galveston to our satisfaction.

We entered the ice cream parlor. It was a large room divided at the center by strips of wood, filled with plants and flowers.

In the first section, there were ice cream machines on both sides of the entrance, and in the second section, countless small, round tables indicated the space for customers and flowers—and there were flowers everywhere, artificial and natural ones. Electric fans mounted on the walls, ceilings and tables cooled the entire area.

Half an hour later, we were traveling on board an electric train toward Houston. It was late in the afternoon when we arrived at the marvelous bridge that transforms the city of Galveston, at the whim of a man, into an island, a cape, or a small peninsula. Suddenly, I saw the sun disappear into the sea. It was divine, Tía. The sky and the water suddenly turned red, and shortly afterward, it looked like everything was going to catch on fire—the coast, ships, clouds, water and sky. Everything looked like an immense fire, traversed, from time to time, by birds which look like fire bullets with wings moving toward the coast because of the red color reflected on them.

The bridge was raised to permit an enormous boat to cross through the canal; we stopped for a while. I saw the bridge man inside his small tower, attentive to the crossing of the ship. When the ship reached the other side, he pulled the lever, and that enormous iron skeleton, more than fifty meters in length, began to descend smoothly. A minute later, we crossed at full speed.

Your niece,

Olga Beatriz.

Letters (English)

✠ Negroes ✠

Tía Ciria:

The last days we spent in Houston, we spent them getting to know the inner city, which in reality is a large and beautiful city. It is situated in continuous contact with Galveston, Texas City, and New Orleans; four steam locomotives leave daily for New Orleans. Two steam locomotives and hourly electric trains depart for Galveston daily. Eight electric trains and two steam locomotives depart for Texas City daily. If to this is added the fact that Houston is the hub of cotton transactions, the secret for its development and wealth will be revealed.

Cotton fields extend into the outskirts of Houston; amidst the whiteness of the cotton bolls, the ebony faces and torsos of the Negro workers stand out, men and women who for centuries have been used to harvest the fiber.

With respect to Negroes—one morning we went through the center of the ghetto where colored people, as they are referred to here, live, and I was horrified. One can hardly imagine worse filth; dirty houses, broken wire fences, amidst dirty yards together with pigs and horses, little black children of all ages are seen lying on animal excrement like gigantic flies coming out of the garbage. In several doors or in several windows or on the sidewalks, big ugly dirty Negro women stand smoking pipes which emit more smoke than a locomotive engine. They go from here to there wearing extravagant dresses, with large, worn out straw hats. The Negroes were wailing in incomprehensible English so that not even the chauffeur could easily understand their language.

"This is a piece of African land," said Papa, and the chauffeur added, "A very large piece since five thousand Negroes live here." These people are so ugly and dirty that Americans are right to segregate them from all white public places, and the segregation goes so far that in the state of Texas, it is a crime for a Negro man to marry a white woman or a white man to marry a Negro woman. In addition to declaring the marriage null and void, the offenders are jailed and severely punished.

In many theaters there are large signs which announce that Negroes are not admitted; the same is true in restaurants, as well as in hotels, in general, in all public places, and where they are allowed to enter, there is a special place for them where they must stay.

This has obligated them to have their own theaters, bars, hotels, casinos, and even neighborhoods which I have described above.

As far as everything else, they are a hard working and untiring people; and, in general, very accommodating to whites, whom they ordinarily consider superior. In all areas of the city, the servants are Negroes. In hotels and restaurants, young waiters are Negroes, and in the rural areas, the majority of the workers are Negroes. I say the majority because they are being displaced by Mexican workers who are more active and less pretentious in terms of salary and have access to all public places; that is to say, they have the same rights as whites.

Of course, Negroes do not look very highly upon Mexicans because in their struggle for survival, they have lost their fight to them; consequently, little by little, they have been displaced—first, from field work and later, from the cities.

Negroes are feared because the majority of crimes committed are committed by Negroes; that is to say that these pieces of live coal whose teeth and the whites of their eyes are the only things visible are hated, frightfully hated by whites, especially by white women, to the extent that in Houston I saw a white lady dust off her skirt because it had been grazed by the skirt of a Negro woman as she walked by her.

Unfortunate Negroes, they carry their blackness even in their luck.

Olga Beatriz.

✣ OTHER BUILDINGS ✣

My Dear Aunt:

Among the principal buildings of Houston that we became familiar with is the Presbyterian Church, located on a corner. Its stone construction has a beautiful four story tower which stands out and the third floor of the tower has several very nice circular stone balconies.

Here Catholic churches are few, because most churches are Protestant. The few that do exist are ugly; they look like rooms that are missing art pieces, even the paintings of the saints are not very good; at least, this is true in the few churches I have seen around here.

Another building worth mentioning is la corte (**Harris County Court House**) where the court rooms and county offices are located. The building is built in the center of a beautiful garden and occupies an entire block.

El Palacio del Ayuntamiento, or **City Hall,** as it is called here, is another of the beautiful buildings of Houston; it has two four-story towers. The last floor has the circular balconies of stone which I mentioned when I spoke of the Presbyterian Church. One of the towers has a clock with four faces, one on each side—such a clock is known to have been installed later, since it was necessary to make some modifications to the original tower; as a result, one side of the tower looks different from the other three sides, and it creates a bad impression, but Americans are not concerned with architectural beauty. This explains why with a few variations, all homes are the same hovels covered with uniform wooden tiles (**shingles**), square windows, and, in the front, they have some *porticos,* or verandas that here are called

Porchs, and with the exception of the color, they are all the same. They all possess the same architectural design.

One afternoon we went to **Houston Heights,** a suburb of the city which is built in the highest elevation of the city. In summary, it has a long wide road with a garden of big trees in the center, and, on the sides, a multitude of plants. The most modern homes of Houston are built here; some stand out because of the novelty of the common "**bungalow**" style of architecture. This place, nevertheless, in addition to the garden which is beautiful, has the added attraction of the cool breeze that is always present since it is situated in the highest elevation of the city and a fairly high esplanade; the breeze kept the bothersome heat of the city away.

I will mention the last thing about Houston, the viaduct and canal. North of **Main Street** is a large bridge under which runs a canal that connects Houston to the Gulf of Mexico. It is several miles long and traveled by vessels of small drafts to transport cotton to the sea.

On one side of the canal are railroad tracks for steam locomotives; on the other side is a highway, well paved for carriages, wagons, and automobiles, so that by standing beside the railings of this bridge, one becomes aware of the tremendous commercial movement in the this city: above, electric trains, wagons, automobiles, carriages, pedestrians—all hurrying: underneath, the canal, small and large gasoline steamships continuously moving and producing the same ta ta ta ta ta ta of the gasoline barges that cross the canals of Xochilmilco.

Once in a while steam locomotives go by pulling forty or fifty cars, and on the other side, the comings and goings of loaded vehicles make one dizzy.

I have mentioned everything, Tía, that is worth seeing in Houston. We saw other things and other houses, but they don't deserve to be mentioned. You must be bored now of Houston, as we were, especially since the heat kept getting hotter and hotter and with it the annoyance.

"Let's go to El Paso," one day Papá exclaimed. We packed our luggage and we were off to the station.

Your niece,

Olga Beatriz.

✛ On Our Way ✛

The Union Station where we were to board the train is a shed of several floors; it is the ugliest and the most monotonous thing that I have ever seen. It looks like the laundry house of Magnolia Street in Mexico City. The building is made of red brick darkened by the continuous varnishings created by the smoke from the locomotive engines.

We entered and a black man marked with the number 6, on a small metal plate that he wore on the buttonhole of his blue uniform, gave us the necessary information to buy our tickets, check in our luggage, and took us to the train station lot—in effect, all that a traveler needs to know. To my curious questions, which my father translated, the black man marked number 6 informed me that there were ten other employees just like him, in charge of providing passengers whatever information they might need up to helping them board the cars of the train with their luggage. They did all of this without a salary of any kind.

At 10:00 o'clock in the evening of July 12, luxuriously accommodated on one of the luxury sleeping cars of the Southern Pacific train, we left Houston en route to El Paso.

The sleeping cars of this train are very elegant, and they are about one third longer than the ones in Mexico City. The beds are wider, so that one sleeps more comfortably, and each compartment has an electric light bulb, recessed in the wall of the car; it is turned on or off by simply opening the little box where the light bulb is located, like the ones that are used in the sleeping cars in Mexican trains that run from Mexico to Veracruz.

Added to the sleeping car is a dining car which I learned about the following morning. This was for me a novelty, since every time we traveled in Mexico, we had been served our meals in the same car in which we traveled on small tables that we attached to the seats.

The dining car, besides being very elegant, is perfectly attended by a white manager and several waiters, or young black men that wait on passengers with solicitous promptness; even miniature plate settings for the children! Imagine, Tía, my sisters, Tarsela and Rojana, were sat in small chairs, given miniature silverware, small glasses, small cups, and even small napkins. It made me think of my doll games; they must be gathering dust in Villa Olga, Mixcoac.

We traveled all day and all night, moving across the state; that's when I became aware of the monotonous landscape: yellow lands, without any form of cultivation that would once in a while alter the terrain and train stations that did not add anything with their presence.

San Antonio, Texas, which is a city of importance, according to what I have been reading, is the most important city between Houston and El Paso, but I didn't even see the train station because we went by it during the early morning hours, and I was fast asleep.

I only saw one thing in front of the Del Rio train station that gave me true joy, the Río Bravo of the North, on whose river bank we traveled for a long time; its waters, muddy and rapid, marked the boundary to my country. It is represented here by rugged, blackish, and unyielding rocks against the fire of the sun, without a tree, without a person, as if trees and people wanted to hide from the destruction of the war and the fire.

At ten o'clock in the evening, our train entered the city of El Paso.

Olga Beatriz.

✠ ABOUT THE HOTEL ✠

Tía Ciria:

The fourteenth of July was the first day we spent in El Paso. I opened one of the windows of our apartment in the Sheldon Hotel which faces the small plaza and tried to orient myself: in front of the hotel was San Francisco Street with a distinct panorama, from an elegant jewelry store to some empty lots. To the right of the hotel stood a large department store and the "Anson Mills" building, the tallest building in El Paso.

This building was built in the same spot where the first house built on this side of the river was built during the Spanish conquest. I learned this information later through an inscription that I read in the entrance that said **"On this spot then—near the river—opposite the ancient—City of Paso del Norte—Juan María Ponce de León— the first settler on this side built this house in 1827."**[1]

This lot was acquired by the American General, Anson Mills, in 1857, but the present building which he named after himself wasn't built until a few years ago. This General still lives.

In the same small plaza are located the offices of *El Paso Herald*, one of two English language daily newspapers that is printed here; a bookstore; the McCoy Hotel; and in the corner of El Paso Street, the offices of a bank. This is what I first saw in the city of El Paso.

I forgot a detail of our arrival that might be of use to travelers. As one leaves the station, there are many automobiles available, sym-

1. En este lugar, entonces cerca del río, frente a la antiguq ciudad de Paso del Norte, Juan María Ponce León, el primer colono en este lado, construyó su casa en 1827.

metrically parked; they wait for passengers—chauffeurs called out to the passengers to take their cars and informed them that they can take them to any hotel in the city for only fifty *centavos* per person. We walked to one of them, but the chauffeur insisted on charging for Rosana, even though she is only eighteen months old, and while we were discussing this matter, a trolley arrived and we took it. We went through several streets to arrive at the hotel. It cost us fifteen *centavos* rather than twenty *reales*.

It occurs to me, in light of this incident, to give passengers a word of advice. It is not wise to take taxis of any kind in the train station; it is best to wait for the trolley since it goes to the center of the city and costs only five *centavos* and once there, one can transfer to another trolley without having to pay extra for the transfer; one only has to ask the driver for some tickets called "**transfer.**"

While my sisters were being dressed, I went out of the hotel to walk around the block; the post office is behind the hotel; the base of the post office building is made of stone and the rest is made of a thin wall. The offices are located in the mezzanine, which can be reached by a stairways, and since it is built on a corner lot, there are two entrances to the building, one on each side of the building, facing the two streets that meet at the corner of the block. The stone stairways are wide but steep and very difficult to climb. As a whole, the building is very charming.

To the east of the hotel is the San Jacinto Plaza, which has in the center a garden with a fenced-in area that houses two large crocodiles which are admired by pedestrians. Close to them and in contrast to them are two small turtles which appear to have become accustomed to living with such tremendous company.

In this same garden is located a tall flagpole which flies the American flag.

Over an artificial cavern stands a small cannon, a historical reminder to the natives of El Paso and posted, next to it, is a notice offering five *pesos* as a reward to anyone who reports and presents proof of an individual damaging the property of the garden.

Consequently, all pedestrians watch one another and, until now, I don't know of anyone who has claimed the five *pesos*, but, at the same time, no one destroys public property in the least iota.

Here, like in Houston, and, I believe, in all American cities, spitting in public places is prohibited. Severe penalties are imposed to avoid the spreading of contagious disease, so the garden has warnings posted, both in English and Spanish, that inform the public.

I returned to the hotel for breakfast, and as I crossed the street, a group of paper boys approached me, shouting the names of the morning papers and among them was *El Imparcial* of Mexico, which reminded me of my beloved country and especially my home in Mixcoac, so far away.

In the **lobby** of the hotel, I bought, following my customary habit, a set of postcards of El Paso and made plans to see the city—my usual tools to familiarize myself with the most interesting and important sites of the city.

Olga Beatriz.

✛ A Bird's Eye View ✛

Tía Ciria,

Lee is the name of the chauffeur of a powerful automobile that we rented to go sightseeing around the city. He is not a vulgar man; he knows history, recounts anecdotes, and retells, more or less, interesting episodes of places that he points out.

The first day he proposed that we tour the city quickly in his automobile, so we left the hotel early and drove around El Paso.

On the first street we had to cross some railroad tracks. Long narrow strips of red wood nailed to small iron columns slowly descended in front of us and we could not continue our tour. Lee explained—my Papá translated—Niña, do you see that small yellow and wooden red tower that's located on the side of the tracks? Inside—look, you can see for yourself—is a man who can, by means of a small lever that at this moment he is holding in his hands, lower the wood barrier that extends across the street and the smaller one that extends across the sidewalk. On those strips, you can read the printed words **"Safety First. Stop. . . Look . . . Listen,"** which indicate that one should consider safety first and to consider safety first, one must "Stop, Look, and Listen" because when a train approaches, the crossway is dangerous, but more than warning us, it prevents us from crossing the tracks. "Thanks to this," he continued, "there aren't very many accidents, and there should never be any accidents, but there are some people that do not stop when they reach the tracks, nor do they look or listen. They go around the wooden barriers and cross the three sets of tracks, and usually their bodies are left behind as pulp on the railroad tracks."

With the speed of lightning, a locomotive went by, pulling sixty cars. This was for me a novelty; the engines are enormous and they have an enormous potential. The one that I saw (and this occurrence has been repeated) was pulling sixty cars filled to the brim.

When the train went by, the barriers were lifted and like an avalanche, cars crossed the railroad tracks; we did too, like other automobiles, carriages, bicycles, motorcycles, and about eighty people who had been delayed from their goings and comings and also crossed the tracks.

"There is in the United States," added Lee, honking his car horn as he crossed the tracks, "a large association here, as everywhere else, that has its delegates make use of all the possible media—movies, conferences, warnings, articles in the newspapers, talk, at church, and personal advertisements—to advocate decreasing unfortunate accidents which are caused by an individual's lack of foresight. Consequently, everywhere you will run into the "**Safety First**" sign, their slogan, which in Spanish means Safety First; that is to say, before one undertakes any action, one should be careful to avoid an unfortunate accident."

We arrived at the Cleveland Gardens, which is one of the prettiest in the city of El Paso—in truth, a city poor in gardens, if it is compared to any Mexican city. The public library is located in the center of this garden. I will speak to you about it later, for now, it is enough to tell you that its entrance is made up of a hall or terrace which has four wide columns which make up its frontage and which resembles the temple of Diana, of Ephesus, that I saw in my *Manual of Universal History*. I can reach this terrace by a wide and comfortable stairway made of stone.

Later, we returned to the Cleveland Gardens and we went by the Masonic Temple, a seven-story building, constructed of cement and dark red brick. In front of the southeast corner of the garden, we passed by the Young Men's Christian Association building, whose frontage has a series of concentric arches that serve only as an entranceway, the rest demonstrates solidity, but not beauty.

Through a street that was sloping, we arrived at **Sunset-Heights,** a neighborhood in El Paso where you find, undoubtedly, some of the most beautiful homes of the city.

The land the city is built on is not flat except in the center of the city. The land has been taken away from the river (and, in passing, from us Mexicans) so the city has extended its building onto the mountains and the nearby hills. Because of their inability to level the land, they have built houses on the mountains and hills, so that there are homes on the peak and in the lower levels of the mountains. All the different designs give this combination certain originality and great beauty. **Sunset-Heights** is like this, and as the previously mentioned houses stand alone, that is, they are not connected to one another, each one having its four sides free, the difference in levels makes them look like a nativity scene during Christmas Eve.

In the center of **Sunset-Heights,** there is a well-kept, rhomboidal-shaped garden, where the streets Porfirio Diaz, **Lawton, Upson, Prospect,** and **West Boulevard** meet; all of the homes are large, beautiful, and elegant.

We stopped for a little while in front of the park, and then we continued through **Prospect Avenue;** we arrived at **Height St.** and followed it in a straight line until we reached the preparatory school (**High School**). We traveled through a series of zigzagging streets, traveling through the **Franklin Heights** neighborhood and through **Highland Park,** until we reached the last houses. From there, we returned through **Manhattan Heights** (another neighborhood), then entered **Montana Street,** which has one of the more modern homes, and followed it for about twenty-five blocks, since it is very long and very well paved, until we arrived at **North Oregon St.,** which took us to the hotel. Dizzy from the parade of houses and streets, I pulled myself together so that I would be able to organize my notes so that later I would be able to write you these lines.

Olga Beatriz.

✛ Incomprehensible Castilian ✛

We moved in.

Our home was a toy, resembling a mission, recently completed. It had five bedrooms and a bath, in addition to the corresponding **"Sleeping Porch,"** where we placed conveniently, or better said, three cots were already there. There wasn't much furniture, but the existing pieces were brand new. Among them was a magnificent piano that half an hour after we moved in, at the promptings of my fingertips, played the ever so beautiful notes of the National Hymn of Mexico. Most likely, it was the first time the strings of its sonorous lungs had been played since it left the factory. I extended our flag over the top of the piano, in the manner of an encasement, and created for myself the illusion of a Mexican conquest.

On the center of the dining room table stood a flower pot which contained an asparagus plant whose leaves draped down the sides of the table. The plant was recommended by the owner of the home like an eye of a face. And to think that in Villa Olga, Mixcoac, we pay so much attention to it.

The house had a telephone, two gas stoves, one wood stove, sufficient cupboards, dishes for cooking, and finally, everything that one might need to live comfortably. In a word, there was nothing extra, but nothing needed to live comfortably was lacking. All of this for forty-five dollars a month. It's not that expensive, is it, Tía?

Among the numerous women who came to apply for the job, we accepted one that assured us that she knew everything there was to know about the kitchen, but, in reality, the poor thing knew very

Letters (English)

little. On the other hand, I learned from her the dialect that the majority of the Mexicans who have lived here for a long time speak.

Because you must know, Tía Ciria, that it is not easy to understand the Castilian of the Texas Mexicans who, because of their contact with Americans, have Mexicanized many English words, and anglicized many Spanish words, to the extent that their dialect is a mixture of Spanish and English, both incorrect, both badly pronounced, and truly incomprehensible.

I will give you an example. One day, the maid did not show up to work in the morning and when she arrived in the afternoon, I asked her why she had been absent. She answered in the following manner, that I suppose it will be difficult for you to translate:

"Yesterday, I was coming from the *Esmelda*, and I asked in the *carro* for a *trance* to go to the *dipo* where I had been told there was a *marqueta*, and I needed to buy some *mechas* and see if there was an inexpensive heater, for which I had enough wood in the *yardita*, but when I was about to arrive, the *traque* broke and I had to wait, so I went to the home of the López family of Chihuahua. The *babis* had torn opened a package of *espauda*, the kind that is used in *bisquetes*. The lady asked me to lend her a *daime* to buy another one, and since I didn't have any other except that one, I had to walk and I became sick. That's why I am late."

Did you understand? You didn't, did you? Well here goes the explanation: *esmelda* is what around here they call the neighborhood where the **Smelter** is located. *Carro* is what they call the *tranvía* because in English it is called **car.** *Dipo* is a incorrect adaptation of **Depot,** which means train station. *Trance* is a ticket that one receives in the trolley to **transfer** to another trolley without paying. I have already mentioned this act in a previous letter, such a ticket in English is called **transfer.**

They use the word *marqueta* rather than *mercado*, which in English means **market;** *mechas* are **matches,** and it has been taken from the English word, **matches.** *Calentón* is a Castilian barbarism, since it is used instead of *calentador*, a kind of portable heater that is used inside a home during the winter. *Yardita* is a Mexican diminutive for the English word **yard** which means **yard** or **corral.** *Traque* is what they call the railroad tracks. *Porcha* comes from the word **porch.** It has been Castilianized and it is those **porches** which I mentioned previously.

Babis is an absurdity for the English word **babies,** which means children. *Espauda* is used instead of **powder** which means baking powder and *bisquete* is a Mexicanization of **biscuits,** which are small sweet breads or small rolls. *Daime* is used by the Mexicans instead of **dime,** which is pronounced "daim" and it is the name of a ten cent silver coin.

Now with these explanations, you should be able to translate the incomprehensible Spanish of Carlota (which is the name of the maid), the same one that the majority of Mexican workers use.

Americans and compatriots need interpreters to understand them!

Your niece,

Olga.

✝ Él Exodo ✝

Tía Ciria:

Amanecía en Mixcoac.[1] Eran las cuatro y media y con el apresuramiento que me daba la alegría de un próximo viaje me desayuné de prisa. Salimos: un tren de San Angel detúvose en la Parada la Candelaria, subimos apresuradamente y vi la "Villa Olga", mi casa querida, perderse entre el tupido cortinaje de los árboles.

Veinte minutos después estábamos en México: en la calle de San Juan de Letrán, de donde un automóvil nos llevó a la estación de Buena Vista. México me parecía más alegre que de costumbre. Hacía mucho tiempo que no lo veía tan temprano: las tiendas cerradas, los coches caminando lentos, los gendarmes bostezando, un perrillo pasó junto a nosotros . . .

En la estación esperaba Cordero ¿ya te acuerdas? el Secretario de papá. Nos metimos al Pullman: yo no podía hablar ¿alegría? ¿tristeza? quizá las dos cosas . . . Esperamos mucho, interminablemente; y por fin el tren empezó a andar, lento primero, después más rápido, de manera que los postes y las casas me parecían correr a todo escape, hacia la ciudad.

Las estaciones todas iguales: jacalones de madera unos, otros de piedra; pero siempre en la misma forma: angulares y nada bellos.

Llegamos a Esperanza, y a comer "algo que no sean latas de Pull-

1. To maintain authenticity to the original text, I have typed this copy exactly as it appeared in the original. I did not correct grammar, usage, or punctuation. Boldface words in the original text remain boldface in my transcription. Boldfaced words in the English translation appeared in English in the original text.

man", había dicho mi papá. Y comimos. El restaurant, está servido por chinos y se compone de un gran salón con mesas paralelas, en torno de las cuales se sientan apresuradamente los pasajeros y se sirven sólos; pues los mozos, ponen en el centro, fuentes con los distintos manjares de la comida y a servirse cada cual . . . había algo bueno; pero no lo probé, se lo llevaron, o más incorrectos o más hambriados que yo. "Al tren de nuevo", dijo un conductor, y siguió la marcha.

A las ocho de la noche llegamos a Soledad y el Conductor del Pullman nos dijo que allí había que dormir y allí dormimos. En tiempos de paz, en otros viajes, habíamos dormido en Veracruz; pero la guerra es mala para todos, hasta para mí que empiezo a vivir.

Hacía un calor insoportable, y desde entonces,—28 de Junio— no hemos dejado de sentirlo en todas partes. Nos salimos de aquel encierro y recorrimos el poblado: en la obscuridad de las calles se veían sobre las banquetas los soldados durmiendo, otros charlaban: "la ciudad es un campamento", me dijo una mujer a quien interrogué.

Al día siguiente trasbordamos a un tren militar en donde registraron el equipaje, se robaron un relojito mío ¿te acuerdas, el de las iniciales? y nos llevaron hasta Tejería. Este era el punto más avanzado de los soldados de Huerta.

Nos habían dicho que de Tejería a Tembladeras (punto avanzado de los americanos) teníamos que viajar a pie; pero mañana te diré cómo lo hicimos porque esta carta está ya muy larga.

Tu sobrina que te quiere,

Olga Beatriz.

✛ En Camino ✛

Tía Ciria:

Te decía en mi anterior, que llegamos a Tejería, a bordo de un tren militar. Allí, poco antes de bajarnos, subieron al tren tres individuos de caras sospechosas, quienes cuidadosamente veían a todos los pasajeros. Uno de ellos se acercó a mi papá y habló con él, enseñándole un telegrama; después se alejó moviendo la cabeza.

Nos bajamos: un teniente de artillería interrogaba a los pasajeros aquí y allá, preguntando si el convoy no había sido asaltado en el camino, si había tranquilidad en México, y otras cosas que, a mi juicio, tenía más obligación él de saberlas que nosotros.

Rápidamente nos subió papá a un carro cubierto con un toldo: cobraron un peso por persona, y faltó espacio para los pasajeros.

Así marchamos rumbo a Tembladeras, dando tumbos, pues seguimos la vía del ferrocarril destruída allí por orden del General Maass, cuando huyó de Veracruz y estaba sembrada de trozos de durmientes quemados.

Hacía un calor de fragua: El paisaje era hermosísimo por más que varias veces lo he visto ya; pero siempre me parece lo mismo, árboles por donde quiera, flores a millares, plantas en todas partes . . .

Se detuvo el carro frente a una tienda de campaña, a cuya entrada estaban un subteniente y cuatro soldados: eran los últimos soldados de Huerta que habíamos de ver. Allí bajamos y seguimos el camino a pie; el carro no podía seguir por la vía, porque un furgón de carga la cubría. Esa caminata fue eterna; más de un kilómetro bajo un sol de fuego, sobre una tierra que ardía, dando brincos de durmiente a durmiente . . . figúrate tía!

Allí esperamos como dos horas: unos hombres venidos de Veracruz vendían limonada a cincuenta centavos !sabían ellas a gloria!

Mientras vendían su mercancía, entretenían a los compradores, con asombrosos relatos de la toma de Veracruz por las fuerzas americanas—de cómo todas las vidrieras de los edificios del centro de la ciudad estaban acribilladas a tiros, de cómo el pueblo de Veracruz al darse cuenta de la retirada del ejército se había reunido en las calles y habían hecho fuego sobre los que desembarcaban; pero como la mayor parte no tenían armas, se contentaban con lanzarles piedras. Contaban cómo los grandes acorazados lanzaban granadas tremendas sobre los edificios, principalmente sobre la Escuela de marina, quedando destruída ésta y en fin, todo lo relataban de manera atropellada produciendo una sensación de horror y de odio hacia los alsaltantes.

Me ví tentada a pedirle que nos regresamos a México; pero el recuerdo de las persecuciones que pretexto de política había sufrido mi papá, los estragos espantosos que las hordas zapatistas hacían en las goteras de la gallarda Ciudad, las venganzas injustificadas de los partidarios del Gobierno, los asesinatos cometidos por misteriosos matadores de personas a quienes se creía desafectas al Gobierno, y en fin, los horrores, que oía contar que iba extendiendo por todas partes la guerra, me hicieron pensar que la vuelta a la Ciudad de los Palacios, sería el más grande de los disparates.

En medio de estas reflexiones que hacía menos larga la espera, se escuchó un silvato y entre la selva, una densa columna de humo negro nos señaló la proximidad del tren.

Llegó éste, llevando en la salpicadera o trompa de la máquina a unos individuos vestidos de kaki y con sombrero de fieltro de anchas alas: cada uno llevaba un fusil al hombro: "¿Quiénes son esos?" pregunté.

"Soldados americanos" contestó mi papá y agregó emocionado "es triste verse obligado por la tiranía a buscar bajo el amparo de estos hombres paz y seguridad . . ."

Subimos al tren y después de caminar largo rato vimos entrar al carro en que íbamos a un médico (después supe que era) y un muchacho con una caja de papeles; ¿qué querían? Unos pasajeros nos dijeron que nos iban a vacunar. !Figúrate! eso no nos gustó mucho; pero ¿que remedio? Sin ese requisito no podíamos llegar hasta el puerto.

Y era de verse a los señores quitarse el saco y poner al descubierto sus brazos lo mismo las señoras. Nos vacunaron a todos mediante unos rasguños que nos dieron en el brazo con unos fierritos y luego nos aplicaron el suero: preguntaron los nombres y nos expidieron el certificado respectivo.

Al llegar a "Los Cocos" a uno y otro lado de la vía, ví el campamento de los soldados americanos: fuertes tiendas de campaña amarillas; y junto a ellas unos salones de madera forrados de tela de alambre y dentro, en largas bancas, frente a angostas mesas, soldados americanos comiendo: aquí y allá, destacamentos hacían guardia . . .

A las doce y media entraba el tren a Veracruz: nuevo registro de equipajes, nuevo ir y venir de cargaderos, gritos aquí, gritos allá, y por todas partes soldados americanos caminaban mudos por la ignorancia del idioma.

Veinte minutos después estábamos en el hotel.

Tu sobrina,

Olga Beatriz.

✠ VERACRUZ ✠

Tía Ciria:

En Veracruz, además de la calamidad del calor, teníamos otra peor: la mala comida; y eso que según oí decir, estaba su calidad en razón inversa del precio: mientras más mala más cara: el pescado podía pasarse, la carne asquerosa, la verdura homeopática.

"Figúrese usted" me dijo el maitré d' Hotel, "con la llegada de los americanos y la falta de vías de comunicación, las lechugas valen treinta centavos, los chícharos sólo en latas los hay y a peso, los huevos valen un real . . . y siguió la lista por este estilo, y era verdad lo que decía.

Hasta el hielo escaseaba a grado tal, que fue necesario traer un barco exclusivamente cargado de hielo desde Galveston, ¡y pensar que todo el día los habitantes de Veracruz necesitamos agua con hielo!

La ciudad era un crisol, de manera que prefería estarme bajo la sombra de las plantas del jardín, o bajo el haz de viento del ventilador eléctrico de mi recámara, que salir por aquellas calles de asfalto ardiendo.

Por lo demás, nada había que ver en ellas, si no eran parejas de soldados americanos vigilando las calles, con el rifle al hombro y caminando con paso uniforme, con el chaquetín de kaki empapado de sudor como si se hubieran mojado intencionalmente.

Otras veces, siquiera había zopilotes por las calles recogiendo la basura; pero ahora con las rígidas disposiciones del jefe militar americano acerca de la limpieza, ni un animalucho de esos se veía en parte alguna.

Una mañana fuí a los baños de mar: una tupida palizada impide la entrada de tiburones a un amplio espacio del mar. Se entra por una rampa en dos partes iguales y en el fondo, perpendicularmente a ella, hay un edificio de madera destinado al Club de Natación y en el cual venden refrescos.

A uno y otro lado de la entrada, sobre la arena, hay unos cartuchos en donde se desnudan los bañistas y se proveen del traje de baño y . . . al agua!

Agradable es el baño en todas partes; pero en Veracruz y estos de mar principalmente, son un pedazo de gloria líquida; y tanta gloria tomé, que estuve a punto de enseñarme a nadar!

En el puerto, en la bocaná y más allá de ella, barcos extranjeros de todas formas y tamaños, vigilando por la seguridad de sus naciones, conté una tarde cuarenta y dos barcos de guerra: la mayor parte, acorazados americanos, que de lejos parecían cuajar la superficie del mar de catedrales flotantes, por lo enorme de sus torres.

Una tarde fuí a la Escuela Naval, y al contemplar las ventanas destrozadas por los cañonazos de los acorazados me pareció que hacían un gesto horrible de cólera, más que para los invasores, para los nacionales que con sus intemperancias someten a la Patria a semejantes pruebas!

En las mañanas, temprano, y ya en la tarde, las calles de Veracruz y el centro principalmente, se veían llenos de soldados y marinos americanos, y no pocos de éstos, españoles, franceses e ingleses que eran ignominiosamente explotados por los vendedores de curiosidades, que se dejaban pedir un ojo de la cara por cada porquería!

Frente a la Dirección de Faros convertida en cuartel americano y a la orilla del mar mandó colocar el General Funston una sillería en donde los vecinos del puerto se solazaban desde el atardecer hasta las diez de la noche, con vistas cinematográficas que también veían los soldados americanos tirados en el suelo. Lo malo que había allí, tía, era la música, la música militar que destrozaba los tímpanos con sus piezas monorítmicas. Si el señor Cerbon, (me lo saludas) mi profesor de piano, los hubiera escuchado . . . !

Entretanto, pasaban los días y no había un solo barco en que marcharnos: todos los que llegaban y se iban, eran barcos de guerra . . . por fin se anunció que llegaría el "City of México" y nos apresuramos a salir de Veracruz.

El día que atracó lo fuimos a ver . . . ¡qué feo, tía! pero no había otro, y era preciso salir de aquel horno citadino que ya nos asfixiaba.

Tu sobrina,

Olga Beatriz.

Letters (Spanish)

✙ El Mar ✙

Querida tía:

Orgullosa de haber nacido en la capital de la República, desearía que todo aquello que lleva su nombre, fuera grande y bello como es ella, pero al barco "City of Mexico", es una solemne porquería que deshonra el nombre.

Yo no conozco muchos barcos pero los he visto en Veracruz otras veces que hemos estado en el puerto, tales como el "Champagne", y "Morro Castle" y algún otro, son cien veces superiores.

Alguien dijo y quizá tenga razón que el "City of Mexico" es un barco exclusivamente de carga y así se explica que sus camarotes, que no llegan a veinte, sean más bien calabozos en donde sufrí lo indecible.

Te diré cómo era el barco: en el centro, bajo la cubierta, se encontraba el comedor que es un cuadrilátero de unos seis metros por diez, en el cual había dos mesas paralelas y angostas y en el fondo entre ellas, un piano, horrorosamente desafinado y viejo.

Al comedor dan acceso las puertas de unos camarotes, lo que me hace creer que el comedor es en realidad un Hall. Por supuesto que esta disposición hacía que a menudo sucediera que estaba uno desayunándose y si se abría alguna de las puertas de esos camarotes, veía una vestirse a los resagados o dormir semidesnudos a los mareados.

Nosotros teníamos el camarote número 5 que era de los mejores, porque estaba situado en un pasillo que atravesaba el barco de lado a lado y tenía dos ventanillas, especie de claraboyas que daban al mar ¡por allí entraba fresco siquiera!

En la cubierta estaba la cámara del Capitán, dividida ahora en dos partes, la mitad ocupaba él, y la otra alquilaba a alto precio a una familia Newman. Sobre esto había todavía otro departamento destinado a la oficina de la telegrafía inalámbrica.

A uno y otro extremo, lo que llaman proa y popa y en la parte baja, había maquinaria, grúas, cables, engranes, etc., y la entrada a las bodegas, que eran todo el cuerpo del barco.

En esta prisión flotante, nos encontramos a las cuatro de la tarde del tres de Junio, hora y día señalados para la partida. La cubierta estaba llena de gente que veíamos desde unas sillas de extensión que había comprado papá en el puerto, formadas de unos palos pintados de amarillo y unos trozos de lona mala.

Yo no sabía si toda aquella gente iba a viajar; pero era demasiada para el barco . . . Dieron las cinco, y seguíamos anclados y las grúas cargando bultos e introduciéndolos a las bodegas, sin cesar . . . las cinco y media y lo mismo . . . las seis, e igual cosa . . . por fin, a las seis y cuarto oí un ruido extraño, me asomé a los lados del barco, y ví por unos agujeros salir chorros de agua: "la hélice empieza a funcionar" me dijo un vecino amablemente.

Como por encanto, los no pasajeros empezaron a bajar apresuradamente y bien pronto nos quedamos unos cuantos sobre cubierta.

La masa del barco empezó a desprenderse del muelle y a dar vuelta porque teníamos la proa hacia el puerto; y ya con ésta rumbo al mar, empezó a alejarse de la ciudad.

De pronto, los pasajeros empezaron a gritar arremolinándose en un extremo del barco; y éste se detuvo frente al crucero español "Carlos V". Fuí a ver: era un pasajero resagado que a bordo de un bote de gasolina venía a todo escape . . . le soltaron la escala, y subió.

Siguió la marcha y allegábamos a la "bocana" que así se llama al punto donde concluye la bahía y empieza el mar libre, cuando nuevos gritos, nuevo arremolinarse de gente . . . y ví otro bote de gasolina,

Letters (Spanish)

otra resagada a quien se le escapaba el barco . . . detúvose éste, soltaron la escala y con trabajos subieron a la señora y su equipaje: un baúl enorme y dos velices. El del bote empezó a gritar que no le pagaban; le había dado diez pesos y quería otros cinco, !hubo que dárselos! y en marcha!

Entretanto, en la playa, centenarse de pañuelos se agitaban despidiéndonos; del barco les contestaban . . . yo también agitaba el mío . . . y lloré pensando en ustedes, tía, que se guedaban allá a sufrir los horrores de la guerra.

Pasamos luego junto a los acorazados, cuyos marinos también nos despedían . . . poco a poco se fué perdiendo la ciudad, las torres, la playa y bien pronto sólo ví agua interminable abajo . . . y un cielo sin fin arriba!

Nunca había yo visto cosa igual: muchas veces en mis lecturas encontré descripciones del mar, más o menos largas, más o menos bellas pero la verdad es que nadie que tenga un poco de alma, siquiera, en el cuerpo puede dejar de admirar tan enorme grandeza.

Y de mí sé decir, que sentí admiración y miedo. Admiración porque el paisaje es grandioso y bello, la luz al quebrarse sobre las olas produce arabescos de colores tan variados, que los que hablan del "mar azul" del "mar verde" están en un error. La luz le dá a la superficie movediza del mar tantos colores, que ni es verde ni es azul, es una infinita variedad de colores, es una policromía admirable. Y sentí miedo también, porque nuestro barco parecía una pluma pequeñísima sobre el lomo movedizo del Océano. Desde lejos se veían acercarse montañas enormes de agua espumosa, que parecía que iban a sepultar para siempre a nuestro barco y cuando ya estaban cerca, la débil pluma de nuestra embarcación subía sobre aquel lomo rugiente, para esperar al otro lado una nueva avalancha . . . y así interminablemente . . .

Abandoné mi asiento sobre cubierta (larga silla de lona, rústicamente hecha) y me acerqué a la barandilla entreteniéndome en ver pasar ola tras ola, como si en carrera alocada, se quisieran alcanzar unas a otras sin lograrlo nunca; y entre el tejido de las aguas, como en un canevá brumoso, veía juguetear y perseguir al barco, peces de distintos tamaños y colores, sin cuidarse al parecer, de la brusca agitación de la superficie.

De pronto empecé a sentir un malestar horroroso . . . me dolía la cabeza . . . sentía náuseas . . . todo lo veía borroso . . . el mal aumentaba por momentos, y entré de lleno en un sufrimiento horrible . . . nunca he sentido nada peor . . . Papá me cargó en sus brazos, bajó conmigo la parada escalinata y me acostó en el camarote.

A poco ví que mi mamá me hacía companía y que mi papá dándonos aire, le decía a Tarsila que le interrogaba qué teníamos.

"El mareo, Tatitos, el mareo. . .

Hasta la próxima.

Olga Beatriz.

✠ La Familia a Bordo ✠

Tía Ciria:

Dos días duré encerrada en el camarote con mi mamá, las dos mareadas horriblemente . . . el segundo día se aumentó mi mal con una angustia espantosa: figúrate que por las ventanillas del camarote, por las que recibía aire en la cara, empecé a ver que el cielo se ponía negro, que grandes relámpagos parecían incendiarlo todo, seguidos de truenos más fuertes que los cañonazos aquellos que escuchamos en el simulacro de Tlacopac.

Luego comenzó a llover a chorros, y el mar se movía de tal manera que parecía iban a trabarse el barco. Este crujía, abriéndose y cerrándose las puertas, como las casas de México, en aquel temblor del siete de Junio de 1911, ¿te acuerdas? Mamá y yo no hallábamos qué hacer. Afortunadamente, pasó por el Corredor Columbus, uno de los meseros que nos servían y le supliqué llamara a mi papá.

Entretanto, una densa neblina nos rodeaba por todas partes, y a cada minuto un agudo silvido de la máquina, que en mí aumentaba el miedo, anunciaba a otros que pudieran estar cerca, el peligro de un choque.

Un marino se metió de pronto a nuestro camarote, un gigantón horrible y fuerte, que traía unas cosas que me parecieron fragmentos de tabla acolchonada, y nos dijo algo en su idioma, dejando debajo de las camas inferiores, cuatro de esas tablas.

¡Después supe que eran salvavidas, por si había naufragio!

Tras él llegó mi papá, acompañado del marino japonés Densa Mori, quien al ver nuestro susto, y traducirle papá la causa de él; nos tranquilizó diciéndonos que aquello no era nada y que duraría una hora . . . y Denza Mori tuvo razón: una hora después, el cielo estaba de nuevo hermosamente azul.

Al tercer día se nos quitó el mareo y subí a la cubierta, ya sin miedo. Pude comer algo; y a las siete de la noche hora de la comida, ya fuí al comedor y empecé a darme cuenta exacta de todos los pasajeros. Supe que todos ellos se habían mareado; pero la mayoría estaba buena ya y comentaban el mareo entre risas.

Por la noche, ví una cosa espléndida: la salida de la luna sobre la inmensidad del mar. Sale enorme, y parece que todas las olas se convierten en plata movediza. Parece que de la luna sale un chorro de "escarcha" de esa que abunda en los nacimientos de Noche Buena. Tan bonito es, que no lo puedo describir; pero imagínatelo . . . !

Todos los viajeros se habían hecho ya de cierta confianza entre sí, todos parecían formar una sola familia: gentes que no nos habíamos visto antes, y que probablemente no nos volveríamos a ver después; pero por de pronto, nos teníamos tal confianza, que parecíamos parientes todos, o cuando menos amigos muy conocidos.

Para que te diviertas un poquito te voy a contar quiénes eran los pasajeros: Figúrate: dos monjas teresianas, una ya grande, catalana y la otra americana; pero hija de padres mexicanos; iban para San Antonio, Texas, como profesoras de un colegio católico: la muchacha iba además a ver a sus padres, que desde hacía cuatro años no los veía, parte de cuyo tiempo pasó en el Colegio Teresiano de Mixcoac ¿te acuerdas de él?

Un señor alto, fuerte: Rafael Elorduy, hacendado rico, pariente del gran músico Ernesto Elorduy, autor de ese "Vals Capricho" que toco y que te gusta tanto.

Se distinguió este viajero, porque desde que entró al barco hasta que desembarcamos en Texas City, estuvo grandemente mareado, reclinado en una silla de extensión, sobre cubierta, de día y de noche. Hablé con él varias veces y me dijo que sus propiedades las tenía en

Zacatecas y no sabía de ellas;—cosas de la guerra! Lo acompañaba un empleado, joven español, alegre y platicador, que todo el día le llevaba "Apolinaris", única cosa que toleraba su estómago.

Iba también un joven Salinas con su esposa y un chiquito de la edad de Rojana, mi hermanita, quien a menudo jugaba con ella. Un capitán de caballería y otro señor moreno y alto, iban a Sonora a reunirse con los revolucionarios. La señora Mavoy, morena mexicana, con dos niños que lloraban de día y de noche, iba en busca de su esposo a Galveston. Esta señora venía de México, en el mismo Pullman nuestro ¿te acuerdas de aquélla que estaba en el asiento cercano al nuestro, cuando nos despedimos?

Viajaban también dos señores Redo, de Sinaloa, uno de ellos con su hijo y el otro alegre y platicador, de voz fuerte, alarmando a las monjitas con problemas de religión. Venía una inglesa con una niña pequeña; iban a tomar en Galveston un barco para Inglaterra; me dijo su nombre; pero no me acuerdo de él.

También el Capitán japonés Denza Mori, el mismo de que te hablo al principio, segundo comandante del "Itzumo".

Venía la familia Newman que iba para Torreón, dos francesas, tres americanos y por último, ya casi al concluir el viaje, conocí a una compañera de escuela, de mi mamá, la señora Clementina Arteaga, de Aguascalientes, que con una niña y cuatro sobrinas iba a Houston, a reunirse con su esposo, el licenciado Calderón ¡pasó la pobre cuatro días de mareo espantoso!

Por fin, el día 7 de Julio se detuvo el barco frente a Galveston y tras larga espera, llegó el médico sanitario, quien se introdujo con el Capitán en la cámara de éste y estuvo hablando cerca de una hora y se fué. Luego supimos que negó el permiso para bajar, que se debía fumigar todo el barco y que hasta el día siguiente examinaría a todos los pasajeros, !figúrate qué angustia, ver el puerto y estar condenados a un día de encierro!

Olga Beatriz

✠ Frente al Puerto ✠

Tía Ciria:

Cuando se supo la decisión del médico sanitario, todo mundo protestaba, hubo quien pensara en burlarse de la disposición y tomar un bote para ir a la playa; pero los conocedores del asunto, los que ya habían viajado otras veces, decían:

"Sí, bajen ustedes; ya verán como además de pasar algunos días de cárcel, pagar una multa y sufrir otras vejaciones, los mandan, si no en este barco, en otro cualquiera a Veracruz."

Ante esta amenaza, las protestas se acabaron, los más entusiasmados para violar la ley, se fueron conformando; y entre cariacontecidos y risueños, cogieron sus sillas plegadizas y a leer o charlar, frente a Galveston que parecía hervir junto al mar.

Entonces supe que era indispensable que el médico sanitario examinara pasajero por pasajero, pues no se permite la entrada a Estados Unidos a ningún enfermo contagioso. Además, me enteré que habíamos de pasar por el examen del Inspector de Inmigración, pues tampoco se permite desembarcar si no lleva cada quien una cantidad de dinero no menor de cincuenta pesos; y es además persona honrada, laboriosa y de buenos antecedentes.

¡Aquí consideran a los pobres tan peligrosos como a los enfermos contagiosos!

Pensaba yo en todo esto, cuando ví un bulto blanco que cruzaba desde la oficina en que se encuentra la telegrafía inalámbrica y caía al mar . . . tras ése, otro y luego otro . . . corrimos a ver: eran tres pasajeros que desde esa altura se lanzaron al mar, a tomar un baño: ¡me dieron ganas de seguirlos, hacía tal calor!

La corriente era tan fuerte, que uno de los pasajeros poco faltó para que no pudiera alcanzar la extremidad de un cable que le tiraron para que se cogiera de él.

El telegrafista, un flaquillo a quien rara vez se le veía la cara, no teniendo qué hacer, pues estábamos frente al puerto, se contagió con la vista de los bañistas y . . . zas! al agua desde una enorme altura, dió tres brazadas y se pegó al costado del barco. Con esto nos divertimos esa mañana, y luego, a sufrir los horrores de la mala comida ¡qué mal se come en aquel barco, por Dios!

Después de comer se reanudaron las protestas de los pasajeros, porque nos condenaron a las exigencias del Inspector Sanitario a pasar un día frente al puerto; y entonces supe el motivo.

El "City of Mexico", había estado un día antes de llegar a Veracruz, en el puerto de Coatzacoalcos y allí, según aseguraban, se habían dado dos casos de fiebre amarilla; y aún cuando ningún pasajero venía de allá, si había desembarcado: uno de Coatzacoalcos a Veracruz, cuatro que llevábamos de viaje y uno de espera: total ¡seis!

Apoco comenzó a salir por todas las ventanillas y escalinatas un fuerte olor a azufre, todos empezamos a toser y a sentir en la garganta carraspera. No había lugar en donde estuviéramos que no sintiéramos síntomas de asfixia: era que desinfectaban el barco, . . . y a nosotros también.

Por la noche, hasta cerca de las diez, pudimos entrar al camarote, por el olor a azufre que aún existía. Entretanto, con la luna que desde el cielo parecía reírse de nuestras peripecies, te envié un saludo ¿lo recibiste?

Al día siguiente a medio día, el barco se dirigió a Texas City; pero la tarde anterior había yo visto la primera cosa que me llamó la atención en Estados Unidos: llegó el ferrocarril a la orilla de la playa y luego el trozo de muelle en que se había detenido, se empezó a alejar de la costa y bien pronto pasó junto a nosotros y pude ver flotando el tren de pasajeros con éstos tranquilamente sentados como si fueran por tierra y la máquina y los carros sobre un tramo de vía que iba remolcado en el tablón o muelle flotante en que ésta se asentaba, por un vapor que iba al lado. Pasó junto a nosotros y siguió a la playa opuesta; llegó a tierra, y la locomotora echó a andar como si tal cosa, por tierra firme.

En Texas City nos examinó el médico (uno a uno, sobre todo, los ojos, separó a dos pasajeros que le parecieron sospechosos; y empezó después el Inspector de Inmigración, a interrogarnos de dónde veníamos y a dónde íbamos y cuánto dinero llevábamos . . .

Luego registró el equipaje con nuevos trámites que parecían eternos, y por último a las cinco de la tarde saltamos a tierra americana! ¡Ya era tiempo!

Olga Beatriz

✛ Texas City ✛

Mi querida tía:

Lo primero que pensé al saltar a tierra y ver a mi alrededor, fué lo siguiente: "¿Y esto es tierra americana?" ¿pero esto es Estados Unidos?

Frente a mí, a derecha e izquierda, se extendía una inmensa bodega de madera, mal hecha y de feo aspecto, de dos pisos, con una serie interminable de puertas numeradas.

El muelle de madera, toscamente hecho, viéndose a través de los tablones que formaban el piso, un andamiaje de vigas enormemente gruesas que se hundían en un agua verdosa y cochina.

Dentro de la bodega gigantesca, (no he visto otra mayor hasta ahora) se veían aquí y allá, agrupaciones de fardos, cajas, costales, etc., y supe que cada una de esas agrupaciones era el cargamento completo de un barco. ¡ Aquí sólo ocupa su cargamento un pequeño espacio de la bodega!

A lo largo de las paredes había unos aparatos rojos para apagar incendios y otros conectados con líneas telefónicas que basta oprimirles un botón para que anuncien a las estaciones de bomberos que hay incendio.

Detrás de la bodega y al rededor de ella, excepto por el mar, se extendían inmensos terrenos salitrosos y feos, semejantes a los que hay en Nonoalco de México, o en Nativitas o San Andrés Tetepilco. Tan parecido que crece en ellos hasta el zacatón terroso que allá crece.

En el mar era otra cosa: barcos de todos tamaños con distintos nombres: unos en inglés, otros en francés, no pocos en alemán, muchos pequeños, en español y en todos ellos, pintores negros embadurnándolos de color por los costados, desde la línea de flotación a la cubierta, encaramados sobre unas tablas sostenidas por cables y balanceándose sobre la superficie del mar, bastante tranquila por cierto.

Arregló mi papá el traslado del equipaje a la estación del ferrocarril que debía llevarnos a Houston, porque mamá hizo ascos a pasar la noche en estos lugares; "pero si aquí no debe haber ni hoteles" . . . había dicho, y yo participaba de sus ideas.

Echamos a andar por dentro de la bodega, entanto que el resto del pasaje siguió a lo largo del muelle; pero por fuera, bajo un sol que quemaba.

Llegamos al fin a la bodega y seguimos un camino terroso y feo; y no digo calle, porque éstas las considero como el espacio de tierra más o menos ancho que sirve para el tráfico y dá acceso a las casas, y aquí no había casa alguna.

Llegamos a la primera, frente al paradero de los trenes eléctricos, y mi desencanto fué mayor: figúrate un jacalón de madera que con divisiones interiores era a la vez habitación y tienda: las puertas estaban cubiertas de tela de alambre, para evitar la entrada de moscas y zancudos. Afuera, una banca de madera algo sucia, era utilizada para esperar el tren. Y aquel "establecimiento" propiedad, entre paréntesis, de un mexicano casado con una alemana, era todo que de edificios había allí.

No pude contenerme más y pregunté: ¿pero esto es Estados Unidos?

Y entonces supe que esta era una población en nacimiento, que hace cuatro años no había nada en aquel lugar, que era un suburbio, un arrabal de Galveston; pero una compañía estableció allí sus muelles y bodegas y entonces se vino en cuenta que aquel lugar iba a ser de gran porvenir, porque era nada menos que el destinado para que, con mayores ventajas que por Nueva Orleans O Galveston, se enviaran todas las mercancías que de Estados Unidos van destinadas a Panamá.

"Verá usted más adentro, niña, la ciudad naciente: estos terrenos tan feos para usted serán una inmensa ciudad dentro de poco" decía el mexicano de la tienda; "hace tres años me instalé aquí y sólo había cien gentes; ahora ya hay ocho mil, sin contar en que hay además diez mil soldados que están esperando de un momento a otro embarcarse para México..."

El tren tardaba y tomamos un automóvil para conocer el lugar, y entonces ví tenía razón el mexicano!

Calles asfaltadas, salpicadas sus aceras de casas aquí y allá, almacenes de ropa, cantinas, hoteles de tres y cuatro pisos, cinematógrafos llenos de gente, boticas, restaurants, cafés, músicas... se veía, de veras, una ciudad naciente, una ciudad que será grande, grande muy en breve!

Por la calle gentes de todas clases: pero predominando entre éllas los soldados americanos que a todas partes entraban y salían, agrupándose con especialidad en las puertas de las cantinas y a las entradas de los cinematógrafos.

De repente un trueno me hizo levantar la cara al cielo. Se había hublado instantáneamente. A ese trueno siguió otro y luego se desató una tremenda tempestad.

Nos habíamos refugiado en un Café, frente a la plaza.

La gente al atravesar la calle alcanzaba la banqueta chorreando agua... de pronto la calle se convirtió en río y se introdujo una avalancha de agua en un cinematógrafo, cuya entrada veíamos desde nuestra mesa.

Las gentes salieron corriendo y se reían de buena gana empapados hasta las rodillas, ¡aquello parecería agradarles!

A las diez de la noche pudimos salir de allí. No llovía ya.

Olga Beatriz

✛ Tierra Adentro ✛

Quince minutos después estábamos a bordo de un tren en marcha hacia "Texas Junction", en donde debíamos trasbordarnos a un tranvía eléctrico que nos llevaría a Houston.

La noche estaba obscurísima, de modo que no me dí cuenta del camino; pero por un viaje que pocos días después hice de Houston a Texas City, ví que en él nada de notable había: terrenos sin cultivar, salitrosos, un campamento de soldados americanos, con sus tiendas de campaña, semejantes a los que te describí cerca de Veracruz, y por último, unos grandes depósitos de petróleo de la Waters Pierce en mitad del camino.

Veinte minutos después estábamos en Texas Junction.

Yo creí que esta era alguna población: pero me voy encontrando con que era una estación pequeña, y como abandonada, porque no había ni empleados, ni nada que hiciera notar movimiento alguno.

Unos avisos que tradujo mi papá, indicaban la manera de detener el tren o tranvía eléctrico que iba a Houston o a Galveston, pues la vía eléctrica va de una a otra de estas poblaciones.

Y el procedimiento no podía ser más sencillo ni más conocido por mí: de día, agitar un pañuelo para que el motorista lo viera, y de noche, prender un cerillo o mover una luz cualquiera.

Bien pronto vimos a lo lejos un chorro de luz del proyector del tren, que bañaba todo el campo y convertía en apariencia, la línea férrea en dos paralelas de fuego. Hicimos la seña y el tren se detuvo.

Era éste un carro bastante grande, dividido por un cancel de cristales, colocado hacia la tercera parte, en donde iban los pasajeros que deseaban fumar, y en las otras dos terceras partes iban los no fumadores y las damas.

Los carros son elegantes, los asientos son de peluche rojo, nuevo y la parte de metal, de un amarillo bronceado, pulido y brillante. Los asientos son semejantes a los de los eléctricos de México, por lo que se refiere a su disposición, pero tienen en las columnitas laterales del carro, unos timbres eléctricos con los cuales, sin molestarse los pasajeros, en tirar del cordón para que pare el vehículo, como en México, toca uno el timbre cuya campana está situada en la plataforma posterior, en donde va el conductor; y éste tira del cordón de la campana de motorista; sólo él puede hacerlo, pues hay prohibición terminante de que los pasajeros lo hagan.

En la plataforma posterior del tranvía hay dos puertas de cada lado, por una de las cuales se baja y por otra se sube, cuyas puertas se cierran inmediatamente que el tren se pone en marcha, y además, se dobla automáticamente el escalón o peldaño de subida; de manera que nadie puede tomar un tren en movimiento, aunque quiera, por falta de apoyo y de entrada.

Al entrar al carro, se paga o se entrega el boleto: nosotros llevábamos los nuestros desde Texas City.

Al entrar ví el carro casi lleno: mi mamá y Tatos se adelantaron: papá y uno de los pasajeros de viaje desde Veracruz, se instalaron en un asiento lateral y yo y una mexicana que también conocí en el barco, nos sentamos en el último asiento a la izquierda del carro, alegrándonos de encontrar un lugar desocupado.

Poco nos duró el gusto: cinco minutos después se me acercó el conductor y me dijo quién sabe qué cosas en inglés, y me enseñaba un letrero suspendido sobre el asiento, en una tabla que decía: "**For Colored**".

El conductor seguía hablándome en inglés enseñándome el aviso, yo contestaba en español: "no entiendo" él insistía: llamé a mi papá y me enteré del caso.

Había que levantarse de aquel asiento porque estaba destinado exclusivamente a "negros" y como les está prohibido sentarse en otra parte, les conservan sus asientos especiales.

En la estación cercana, una pareja de negros subió al tren y se instaló alegremente en mi antiguo asiento: "**Oguita,** me decía Tatos, viendo con horror a los negros, ¿qué te quitaron tu asiento esos monos tan **negros?**"

A las once y media llegamos a Houston . . .

Tu sobrina,

Olga.

✛ HOUSTON ✛

Querida tía:

Descendimos del tren eléctrico en la calle principal de Houston, llamada "Main Street", al pie de un edificio: el Hotel Rice, tan enormemente alto, que no obstante que la calle estaba muy iluminada, la parte alta de él se perdía entre las sombras de la noche. Cuando de día pude ver este edificio, ví que tenía diecisiete pisos.

Junto a ese y enfrente, y a todos lados, se elevaban otros edificios, si no tan altos como el Rice; sí de ocho, diez y doce pisos; de manera que mi primera impresión fué la de encontrarme en una enorme tumba, cuyas paredes laterales se perdían en el espacio.

Nos instalamos en el Hotel Bristol: hacía un calor insoportable a grado tal, que abrí las ventanas de mi cuarto y eché a andar el ventilador eléctrico. De paso te diré que las ventanas de los edificios americanos, por regla general, no tienen esas hojas de madera que en México se llaman obscuras ni se abren sobre los lados como allá; sólo tienen vidrios colocados de la siguiente manera: la mitad superior de la vidriera está fija, en tanto que la inferior se sube sobre la primera y así queda abierta la ventana; pero no del todo, porque en la parte exterior hay otra tela de alambre, que impide la entrada de los insectos.

A la mañana siguiente, después del desayuno, tomamos un automóvil. Cobran éstos tres pesos por hora.

Y como por la pantalla de un cinematógrafo empecé a ver pasar la ciudad, oyendo las explicaciones que daba el chauffeur y que traducía mi papá. En algunas partes nos deteníamos y entrábamos a los edificios para concerlos.

Así ví aquella mañana el "Banco Nacional del Sur de Texas" cuya fachada la forman cuatro columnas gigantes sobre las cuales descansa un enorme triángulo de mármol, de toda la amplitud de la fachada.

El edificio "Carter" destinado a despachos, es una mole de dieciséis pisos con más de seiscientos despachos; el edificio del Primer Banco Nacional "**First National Bank**", tiene toda la parte baja de mármol, así como toda la parte interior, que es verdaderamente elegante. El Correo es un edificio que ocupa, con el jardín que lo rodea, una cuadra, pero no es tan bello, ni tan elegante como nuestra Dirección General de Correos en México.

Te diré: casi todos los edificios son de monótona arquitectura, son enormes moles cuadradas, salpicadas de ventanas rectangulares que me hacen pensar en palomares gigantesco, sin arte alguno o, sin belleza de ninguna clase . . . te aseguro que mi "Villa Olga" es cien veces superior en hermosura y en elegancia, a estos "palomares" que no tienen sino una cosa verdaderamente admirable, su inmensidad . . . Fuera del centro comercial y a lo largo de la calle principal (Main Street) empienzan las residencias de los ricos de Houston; muchas de las cuales si son verdaderamente hermosas y de un lujo inusitado.

Entre las calles, pavimentadas de asfalto y la banqueta, hay prados de pasto inglés y una interminable arboleda que presta sombra a los peatones y le da un aspecto de hermosura a toda la calle.

Las casas están rodeadas de plantas y pasto por todos lados, y como no hay división entre ellas cada cuadra es un jardín encantado. Mayor idea te formarás de esto si te imaginas que aquí no se acostumbra que vaya una casa pegada a otra como en México, sino que cada una de ellas es un edificio aislado, y el espacio que queda entre una y otra es una prolongación del jardín que tienen al frente.

"Aquí vive un archimillonario de Nueva York", dijo el chauffeur señalándonos un gran palacio de mármol que ocupa media cuadra, rodeada de uno de los jardines mas hermosos que he visto; "pero sólo viene a vivir aquí uno o dos meses del invierno, el resto del año, solamente vive en él la servidumbre".

Y así, deteniéndonos aquí y allá, siempre a lo largo de la "Main Street" desembocamos a una calzada, al final de la cual, hallamos el Instituto Rice. Ese merece carta aparte.

Tu sobrina,

Olga.

✠ El Instituto Rice ✠

Tía Ciria:

Nos quedamos en mi anterior en la entrada del Instituto Rice. Es este un colegio compuesto de varios edificios gigantescos, construídos aquí y allá, sobre una inmensa extensión de terreno destinado al efecto; algunos de los cuales están ya concluídos y otros estarán muy en breve, pues trabajan en ello centenares de hombres.

Será el Instituto Rice un Colegio, en donde los alumnos de ambos sexos, (pues va a haber departamento para mujeres) podrán estudiar lo que quieran: desde la Escuela Primaria hasta la Profesional; porque se podrán estudiar Leyes, Medicina, Ingeniería y Artes Liberales; todo absolutamente gratis, pues el señor Rice, además de gastar diez millones de dollars o sean cuarenta millones de pesos mexicanos ahora; ha destinado para el mantenimiento de dicho Instituto, el producto de otra cantidad no menor que esa.

El señor Rice se propone hacer que den los cursos en su escuela los mejores profesores americanos, según allí nos informaron; de manera que este Instituto, será dentro de poco, según supongo, una de las mejores Universidades de la Unión Americana.

Nos contaron la historia de este raro desprendimiento: el señor Rice, residente en Nueva York, vino a Houston en busca de salud, la cual rápidamente halló; y halló otra cosa: una americanita inteligente con quien a poco se casó. Invirtió más tarde parte de su capital en tierras de Houston, que fraccionó, las cuales le produjeron algunos centenares de miles de pesos. De manera que ha querido pagarle a Houston con ese desprendimiento, el haber encontrado en esa ciudad, salud, felicidad y riqueza.

Letters (Spanish)

Así me lo contaron, y así te lo cuento; pero el hecho es que el Instituto Rice es una de las cosas más notables de Houston; y una de las que más me han llamado la atención. Al caer la tarde, salimos de este colosal centro de educación y a toda máquina nos fuimos al "Parque Colonial". Es semejante al Parque Luna de México, teniendo de notable una grande colección de animales vivos entre los que figura, en primer término, una variada colección de cocodrilos, desde un decimetro de tamaño, hasta cuatro metros, cuya escamosa piel y tremendo hocico, hacen estremecer de horror.

Ví también unas focas de etro y medio de longitud, cuyos cuerpos grasosos y negros, flotaban y se hundían en mil curvas, en un estanque del tamaño de un cuarto.

En unos departamentos había unos avestruces más bonitos que los de Chapultepec, porque lucen todo su plumaje íntegro. Había además una horrorosa colección de víboras varios osos, innumerables changos, dos tigres, y hasta un loro mexicano, según decía el cartel puesto sobre la jaula; cuyo loro zalameramente se despidió de nosotros, diciendo "good bye".

Ya entrada la noche, llegamos a "City Park" que es uno de los jardines mas pintorescos de Houston, por su forma accidentada, atravesado por un riachuelo artificial, cruzado aquí y allá por puentes rústicos, rodeados de pasto inglés

El parque es grande y tiene varios cenadores artísticos, también de forma rústica, en los cuales con avidez grandísima, comían americanos y americanas grandes rebanadas de sandía, suculenta y buena, que les vendía diligente un mexicano, en cuyo puesto de campaña, se leía sobre un trapo **"Watermelons five cents a slice"** (sandía a cinco centavos rebanada).

Un grupo de chiquitines jugaba sobre el pasto inglés, sin miedo a los policías; aquí en lso jardines juegan los niños y se acuestan los grandes, bajo los árboles, sobre el césped, y nadie los molesta "para eso se hicieron los jardines públicos" nos había dicho el chauffeur".

Ya en plena noche, llegamos al Hotel, atravesando de nuevo la "Main Street" que es la Avenida de San Francisco en esta ciudad americana, profusamente iluminada por candelabros como los de aquella vía pública de mi querida México!

Olga Beatriz.

✠ Rumbo al Mar ✠

Tía Ciria:

Una mañana,—el 11 de Julio—amaneció haciendo un calor insoportable, a grado tal que los muebles, las paredes, el piso, todo parecía haber estado junto al fuego, pues se sentían calientes. Un pasajero llegado de Galveston, nos refirió que en ese puerto el calor era tolerable; y resolvimos salir para Galveston.

Puede irse a este puerto por ferrocarril o por tren eléctrico, sin contar que también en automóvil es fácil hacer el viaje; porque a pesar de la distancia que hay, existen calzadas magníficas para automóviles. Nosotros optamos por el eléctrico.

Tómase éste en la calle principal de Houston, una de cuyas casas es la Estación, formada de una gran sala, a cuyo frente hay una doble hilera de bancas, destinadas a comodidades de los pasajeros; y en el fondo se encuentra el expendio de boletos. También en estación, como en el tren, hay unas bancas destinadas a los negros con el famoso letrero **"For Colored"**.

Cinco minutos de espera y llegó el tren eléctrico, el cual hace viajes cada hora rumbo a Galveston. Te dije en una de mis anteriores, que estos carros son muy elegantes, y en este viaje tuve ocasión de comprobarlo. A toda velocidad salimos de Houston, pues estos trenes corren con mayor rapidez que los de Tlalpam en México; de manera que íbamos devorando millas (aquí no se usan kilómetros) en descenso gradual rumbo a la costa. Mientras corríamos, me enteraba de algunos datos históricos de Galveston, de los cuales, te citaré los que más resaltan:

Galveston se llama así, en honor de un Virrey de México, el Conde de Galvez, en cuya época desembarcaron algunos exploradores españoles en este lugar, que es una isla. Más tarde, el famoso pirata Jean Lafitte convirtió esta isla en Cuartel General; y aquí traía todos los productos de sus robos en las costas del Golfo, y es fama que aquí enterró todo el oro que pudo adquirir en un asalto que les dió a unas galeras españolas que llevaban el precioso metal de Veracruz a la Península Ibérica. Esto pasaba en 1816.

Cuando Texas se declaró independiente de nuestra Patria, un coronel, Miguel B. Menard compró a la República Texana, por una friolera, todo el lugar que ocupa la ciudad de Galveston; lo que indica que en esta época, 1836, esta isla estaba desierta todavía.

Al año siguiente, se había dado tanta prisa el coronel Menard en colonizar estos sitios, que se hizo necesaria la construcción de una especie de puerto, y por lo tanto, una aduana, la cual construyó el primer muelle, cuyos trabajos los realizó el Coronel Amosa Taylor.

Sobrevino la guerra civil en los Estados Unidos y a Galveston le tocó su parte de sufrimiento, porque fué bloqueado por la flota Federal. Más tarde, el 1ro., de Enero de 1863, se libró una batalla cerca de Galveston; y por último, fue tomada la ciudad en Junio de 1865.

Estos son los datos históricos más importantes de Galveston, ciudad que como tú comprendes es relativamente nueva.

El camino de Houston a Galveston está bordeado de pueblecitos más o menos hermosos, en la mayor parte de los cuales, se dedican los habitantes a la explotación de huertas y hortalizas.

Bien pronto los manchones de las huertas empezaron a desaparecer, siendo substituidas por terrenos arenosos anunciadores de la cercanía de la playa; y no tardamos en ver las aguas del Golfo.

De pronto, siguió el tren caminando sobre una de las cosas más notables que he visto; una calzada construída de cemento, que une la tierra firme con la isla en que se halla situada Galveston; cuya calzada la forman una inmensa serie de puentes bajo los cuales pasan las olas del mar en vertiginosa carrera, rumbo a la playa.

Esta calzada-puente, tiene más de dos kilómetros de larga y en el centro de ella, hay cosa realmente asombrosa: un puente de fierro levadizo, que cuando van a pasar trenes, automóviles o peatones, cubre el abismo del mar y cuando viene un barco, para que este pueda pasar al otro lado, mueve un sólo hombre, sin esfuerzo, desde una torrecilla de madera, una pequeña palanca, y la masa enorme del puente se levanta suavemente como si fuera de paja y deja el paso abierto a los más grandes vapores. ¡Esto sólo visto, puede creerse!

Semejante maravilla costó dos millones de pesos oro.

Aún no salía yo de la admiración, cuando entraba el tren eléctrico a la ciudad de Galveston.

Mañana te hablaré de ella.

Tu sobrina.

Olga Beatriz.

✝ Galveston ✝

Tía Ciria:

Se entra a Galveston siguiendo un gran jardín en que predominan las palmeras, primorosamente cuidadas, limitado a uno y otro lado por elegantes y ricas residencias, entre las cuales hay algunas verdaderamente hermosas. Descendimos en la estación de los eléctricos que no tiene nada de notable, pues consta de una especie de gran cochera, bajo cuyo techo se detienen los trenes, y a cuya izquierda se encuentra el expendio de boletos con igual distribución que el de Houston.

Me dirigí en seguida a un expendio de periódicos y tarjetas postales en donde me proveí de estas últimas, referentes a los principales sitios de la ciudad.

De paso te diré cuál es el sistema más práctico para conocer las ciudades americanas, y en general las de todas partes, pues hasta en las mexicanas nos ha dado resultado: inmediatamente que se llega hay que comprar una colección de tarjetas postales de la población que se visita, con lo cual se logra tener rápida idea de cuáles son los edificios principales o los lugares más pintorescos. En seguida toma uno un coche o un automóvil (aquí sólo hay automóviles), y se le indica al cochero o chauffeur en su caso, que desea uno conocer lo que las tarjetas postales reproducen. Así se evita uno de guías molestos y carros, según dice papá, que son el terror de todos los viajeros, porque se ponen de acuerdo con cocheros y chauffeurs para aumentar el precio y alargan interminablemente el conocimiento de las ciudades.

Siguiendo ese sistema, tomamos un automóvil, el cual nos llevó a lo largo de la "Market Street", que es una de las calles principales, atravesamos el parque de la ciudad (City Park) en el cual se levanta un monumento en honor de los soldados y marinos de los Estados Confederados, muertos durante la guerra civil; el cual consta de una gran piedra cuadrangular de granito, en la cual se levanta otra de la misma clase, en forma de un cubo, de dos metros por arista, toscamente labrada y sobre la cual se encuentra la estatua de un soldado americano con el pabellón de las estrellas enredado en el brazo izquierdo, y en la mano derecha un rollo de papel, en vez de arma.

Salimos del Parque, atravesamos algunas otras calles y llegamos a una inmensa calzada que limita el mar. Este es el lugar indudablemente más hermoso de Galveston.

Esta calzada es de concreto, pavimentada con unos pequeños bloques de tabique comprimido perfectamente unidos que dan la impresión de que están hechos de madera, tan bien nivelada y perfecta, que el automóvil se desliza sin el más ligero brinco, como si lo hiciera sobre una plancha de mantequilla.

A un lado de esta calzada que mide cinco millas de largo y que costó millón y medio de pesos; se extiende la ciudad con sus alegres casitas del tipo que llaman aquí "bungalow" cuajadas de plantas y flores; y al otro lado, el Golfo de México cuyas últimas olas vienen a morir, convertidas en espuma a unos cincuenta metros de la calzada.

De trecho en trecho se levantan desde la calzada hasta unos cuantos metros adentro del agua, las casetas de madera para los baños de mar entre las que predomina una llamada "The Breakers"; que desde lejos tiene gran parecido con las tribuna del hipódromo de La Condesa.

El más concurrido de los baños de mar es el "Surf Bathing" en el cual, cuando nosotros pasamos, había más de trescientas personas bañándose, entre mujeres, hombres y niños, que lucían los más extravagantes y pintorescos trajes de baño de chillantes colores.

El aspecto es primoroso: figúrate, Tía: unos bañistas, sosteniéndose de unos cables contra el empuje de las olas, otros alcanzados por estos en su fuga hacia la playa y derribados sobre la arena, otros tendidos sobre ésta, y sepultadas de repente por la espuma de las últimas olas. Aquí y allá, grupos de muchachos que de repente desaparecen entre las olas, para volver a aparecer chorreando agua cuando aquellas se van. Y en todas partes gritos, risas y alegría sin fin!

Poco a poco fuimos dejado detrás de nosotros todos los baños de mar al final de la inmensa calzada encontramos un campamento de soldados americanos con sus típicas tiendas de campaña de color amarillo; y más adelante, ocultos entre cerritos artificiales que cubre un pasto verde, unos enormes cañones destinados a la defensa de la ciudad.

De regreso al poblado, seguimos por un camino tepetatoso a cuyos lados había montones de palos y restos de tiendas en completo desorden, como si el mar hubiera destruido un gran ranchería, y apilado aquí y allá los restos de las chozas. Pregunté qué era: "restos de un campamento de soldados americanos, de los enviados a Veracruz", nos dijo el chauffeur, mientras hacía resoplar el ventilador del automóvil.

Hasta la próxima.

Tu sobrina,

Olga Beatriz.

✠ La Ciudad ✠

Tía Ciria:

Por calles feas, en que el agua se había encharcado, durante las últimas lluvias y empezaba a tomar un aspecto verdoso, llegamos al muelle de Galveston, más bien dicho, a los muelles, pues son varios y todos cortados por el mismo patrón del de Texas City: es decir, son largas calzadas de madera, limitadas por el mar, a un lado y al otro por bodegones interminables. ¡Ni Galveston, ni Texas City, no obstante ser de un tráfico marítimo mayor, tienen un muelle con el último de Veracruz.

Eso sí, barcos mercantes, de todas clases y de todas las naciones del mundo, según se ve por la variedad infinita de sus banderas y de sus marinos. Junto a los grandes barcos se deslizan como pequeños peces de colores innumerables botes de gasolina, unos destinados a carga, toscamente labrados, y otros para pasajeros, primorosamente acabados, con los asientos en hilera, a ambos lados y más altos que la cubierta.

Por todos lados un ir y venir de gentes trabajando, que marean; unos apilando mercancías a las puertas de las bodegas, otros cargando carretillas y corriendo con ellas, más allá, grúas levantando pesados bultos para meterlos al interior de los barcos, en otros lados, carros cargados con mercancías, pero en tal cantidad, que parecen casas movedizas, automóvil de carga con ruedas de hule sólidas y dobles, que hacen andar pesadas cadenas, con gran ruido; y entre aquel continuo trabajar en el que se mezclan negros y blancos y morenos; es imposible andar sin peligro de un empujón o de atropello. Aquí, tía, todos van como dice mi papá Julián cuando se enoja: "a su negocio! a su negocio!"

Cuando nos alejamos de allí, mareados de aquel tráfico, habían ya encendido el faro "Bolívar", no obstante que había sol todavía. Este faro es una torre de hierro, forrada de lámina, de forma cilíndrica y pintado a grandes bajas rojas y blancas, terminando con el foco de luz. La torre mide unos veinticinco o treinta metros de altura y aseguran que el alcance del faro es enorme.

Vueltos a la ciudad, nos detuvimos un momento frente a la Estación Unión, semejante a la del Nacional de México, sólo que ésta es de varios pisos. Una cosa me llamó la atención y fué ver una escalera de fierro sencilla, que por el frente de la fachada une todos los pisos; pero demasiado incómoda y peligrosa, para que fuera la escalera principal. Esta misma disposición había yo visto en los edificios altos de Houston y de Texas City; pero no tan perceptible como aquí que afea la fachada, y se me dijo al preguntar, que como son muy frecuentes los incendios en Estados Unidos, estas escaleras sirven para que los habitantes de estos "palomares" tengan fácil escape a la hora del peligro.

Pasamos por la Corte ("Court House") que es el lugar de los tribunales, edificio muy bonito que rompe la monotonía de las demás casas, y seguimos por otras calles hasta entrar de nuevo a la "Market Street" (Calle del mercado) en donde, frente a una nevería, abandonamos el automóvil: cuatro pesos y medio nos había costado conocer a nuestras anchas la ciudad de Galveston.

Entramos a la nevería: era ésta un salón grande dividido en el centro por pequeñas tiras de madera, cubiertas de plantas y de flores.

En el primer departamento, a ambos lados de la entrada estaban los depósitos de nieve y en el segundo; innumerables mesitas circulares indicaban el lugar de los consumidores y flores, y flores por donde quiera: artificiales y naturales pero en las paredes, en el cielo, en las mesas . . . ventiladores eléctricos enfriaban la atmósfera desde los cuatro rincones.

Media hora después, estábamos en marcha, a bordo del eléctrico, en dirección a Houston. Caía la tarde, cuando llegamos al puente maravilloso que convierte al capricho del hombre en isla o en cabo, o en pequeña península, la ciudad de Galveston, cuando vi sobre el mar hundirse el sol: Eso es divino, tía, se van poniendo el cielo y el agua rojos de repente y a poco, parece que todo se va a incendiar: la costa, los barcos, las nubes, el agua, el cielo; todo es un inmenso incendio, cruzado de cuando en cuando por pájaros que por el tinte rojo que reciben parecen balas de fuego, con alas huyendo hacia la tierra.

El puente estaba levantado porque pasaba por el canal un barco enorme y nos detuvimos un poco: vi al "hombre del puente" metido en su torrecilla, atento al paso del barco; y cuando éste estuvo del otro lado, tiró de la palanca, y aquel enorme esqueleto de fierro, de más de cincuenta metros de largo, empezó a descender suavemente sobre él a toda velocidad.

Tu sobrina,

Olga Beatriz.

✚ Los Negros ✚

Tía Ciria:

Los últimos días que pasamos en Houston, los pasamos en conocer el fondo de la ciudad, que es en verdad una grande y bonita población. Está situada en contacto continuo con Galveston, Texas City, y con Nueva Orleans, para donde salen cuatro trenes de vapor diarios. Para Galveston hay eléctricos cada hora, y dos de vapor al día y para Texas City, ocho trenes eléctricos y dos de vapor al día. Si a esto se agrega que Houston es el centro de las transacciones algodoneras, se descubrirá el secreto de su desarrollo y riqueza.

Hasta las cercanías de Houston se extienden los plantíos de algodón, en los cuales, entre la blancura de los capullos de algodón, destacan las caras y torsos de ébano de los trabajadores negros, hombres y mujeres que por centenares, se ocupan en cosechar la fibra.

A propósito de negros: una mañana pasamos por el centro de una barriada de gentes de color, como les llaman aquí; y me quedé aterrorizada; apenas se puede imaginar cochinada mayor; unas casas sucias, con el alambrado roto, entre patios asquerosos, en donde junto a los marranos y los caballos, se miran, tirados sobre el esti-rol, chiquillos negros de todos tamaños, que parecen moscas gigantes salidas de aquel montón de materias en putrefacción. En unas puertas o en algunas ventanas, o sobre las aceras, negrasos cochinos, fumando sendas pipas de donde sale más humo que de una locomotora; y yendo de aquí para allá con extravagantes vestidos y con sombreros de paja enormes y rotos, los negros ahullan un inglés ininteligible, puesto que ni el chauffeur podía entenderles con facilidad.

"Este es un trozo de tierra africana" dijo papá, y el chauffeur agregó: "bastante grande, pues viven aquí cinco mil negros".

Son estos prójimos gente tan fea y tan sucia, que hacen bien los americanos de segregarlos de todo centro de blancos; y la segregación llega a grado tal, que aquí y en general en todo el Estado de Texas, es un delito que un negro se case con una blanca o un blanco con una negra; de manera que además de declararse nulo el matrimonio, los contrayentes son puestos en la cárcel y severamente castigados.

En muchos teatros hay grandes letreros anunciando que no se admiten negros, en los restaurants lo mismo, así como en los hoteles, y en general, en todos los lugares públicos, y en donde son admitidos tienen un lugar especial; del cual por ningún motivo pueden pasar.

Esto ha dado por resultado que se vean obligados a tener ellos sus teatros especiales, cantinas y fondas, casinos y hasta colonia especial, que es la que te describo más arriba.

Por lo demás, son gente trabajadora e incansable y en general, muy serviciales con los blancos, a quienes de hecho consideran superiores. En todas partes, la servidumbre es negra. En los hoteles y restaurants, los mozos son negros, y en el campo, la mayor parte de los trabajadores son negros; y digo la mayor parte porque han empezado a desalojarlos de allí los trabajadores mexicanos que son mas activos, menos pretenciosos por lo que respecta a sueldo y tienen entrada libre a todas partes, es decir, tienen todos los derechos de los blancos americanos.

Por supuesto que los negros no ven con buenos ojos a los mexicanos, porque en la lucha por la vida, tienen con perdido el pleito; de manera que poco a poco van a ir siendo desalojados primero de los campos y luego lo serán de las ciudades.

Los negros son temidos porque la mayor parte de los crímenes que se cometen por aquí, resultan ser hechos por negros, de manera que estos trozos de carbón viviente, en donde sólo los dientes y el fondo de los ojos es banco, son odiados, espantosamente odiados por los blancos; y especialmente por las mujeres, a grado tal, que vi en Houston a una señora sacudirse la falda, porque pasó junta a ella una negra, cuya falda tocó la suya.

¡Infelices negros, llevan la negrura hasta en la suerte!

Olga Beatriz.

✝ OTROS EDIFICIOS ✝

Mi querida tía:

Entre los edificios principales de Houston que conocí, figura la Iglesia Presbiteriana, situada en esquina, y es una construcción de piedra, sobre la cual se destaca una hermosa torre de cuatro pisos, el tercero de los cuales tiene unos bacones de piedra circulares, muy bonitos.

Aquí son pocas las iglesias católicas, pues ésta es protestante, y las pocas que hay son feas, parecen salones en los cuales escasean las obras de arte, pues hasta las pinturas, de los santos no son muy buenas, cuando menos en las iglesias católicas que hasta ahora he conocido por aquí.

Otro de los edificios dignos de citarse, es la corte (Harris Country Court House) que es donde están los tribunales y las oficinas del condado. Es de cantera, muy elegante, en el centro del cual se destaca una gran cúpula, semejante a la que he visto en fotografías que corona el Capitolio de Washington. El edificio está situado en medio de un gran jardín y ocupa con este una cuadra entera.

El Palacio del Ayuntamiento, o City Hall, como aquí le llaman, es otro de los edificios hermosos de Houston, tiene dos torres de cuatro pisos, el último de los cuales afecta la misma forma de balcones circulares de piedra, volados, de que hago mención en la iglesia presbiteriana. En una de las torres hay un reloj con cuatro carátulas, una para cada lado, cuyo reloj se conoce que fué colocado después, pues fué necesario hacerle unas modificaciones a la torre primitiva, lo que dió por resultado, que no se ve igual a la otra, y produce una mala impresión; pero los americanos no se preocupan de la belleza arquitectónica; y así se explica que con ligeras variantes, todas las casas sean iguales, jacolones techados de una teja de madera (shingles) uniforme, ventanas cuadradas y al frente porticos o terrazas que aquí llaman Porchs, y con que excepción del color, afectan todas la misma forma.

Una tarde fuimos a "Houston Heights" que es una prolongación de la ciudad, construída en la parte más alta de ésta, y es en resumen, una larga calzada en cuyo centro hay un jardín, de grandes árboles y multitud de plantas, a los lados, las casas más modernas de Houston, algunas de las cuales sobresalen por su novedad dentro del tipo común de los "bungalows". Este lugar tiene, sin embargo, además del jardín, que es hermosos, el atractivo del aire fresco que en él se recibe, puesto que, como está colocado a mayor altura que la ciudad y en una explanada bastante alta, el aire allí le quita a uno el fastidio del fuego de horno de la ciudad.

Te citaré por último, de Houston el viaducto y el canal: Al Norte de la Main Street, hay una gran puente bajo el cual cruza un canal que une a Houston con el golfo de México, de manera que tiene algunas leguas de distancia y es empleado por barcos de pequeño calado, que trasladan el algodón al mar.

A un lado del canal hay una vía férrea para los ferrocarriles de vapor, y al otro una calzada bien pavimentada para coches, carros y automóviles; de manera que deteniéndose en la barandilla de este puente, se da uno cuenta del gran movimiento comercial de esta ciudad; arriba, trenes eléctricos, carros, automóviles, coches, peatones, todos apresuradamente caminando; y abajo, el canal, surcado continuamente por vapores pequeños y grandes de gasolina, que producen, agrandado, el mismo ta-ta-ta-ta-ta-ta de las lanchas de gasolina que cruzan allá los canales de Xochimilco.

De cuando en cuando pasan trenes de vapor remolcando de cuarenta a cincuenta carros; y por el otro lado, un ir y venir de vehículos cargados que marea.

Te he contado, tía, lo más notable de Houston; vimos otras cosas y otras casas, pero no mercen ser citadas; de manera que fastidiada has de estar ya de Houston, como nosotros lo estuvimos, más cuando día a día aumentaba el calor y con él el fastidio.

"Vámonos al Paso" dijo mi papá una tarde, alistamos las petacas y a la Estación.

Tu sobrina,

Olga Beatriz.

✠ En Marcha ✠

La Estación Unión, en donde debíamos de tomar el tren, es un jacalón de varios pisos; pero lo más feo y monótono que he visto, se parece a la vanadería de la calle de Magnolia en México. El edificio es de ladrillo rojo tirando a negro, por las continuas barnizadas que el humo de las locomotoras le ha dado.

Entramos: un mozo negro, marcado con el número 6, en una plaquita de metal que llevaba en un ojal de su uniforme azul, nos dió los datos necesarios para comprar los boletos, poner el equipaje, lugar por donde debe entrarse al patio de la estación; y en fin, todo lo que un viajero necesita saber. A preguntas curiosas mías, hechas por conducto de mi papá, me enteró el negro "6" que había diez empleados como él, encargados de suministrar a los pasajeros cuantos datos necesitan hasta ponerlos en los carros del tren, con sus equipajes, todo ello sin estipendio de ninguna clase.

A las diez de la noche del domingo 12 de Julio, muellemente acomodados en uno de los lujosos carros dormitorios del Ferrocarril Southern Pacific, salimos de Houston rumbo a El Paso.

Los carros dormitorios de este Ferrocarril son muy elegantes, y como una tercera parte más largos que en los ferrocarriles de México, las camas más anchas, de manera que se duerme mejor, y cada departamento lleva un foco de luz eléctrica, incrustado en la pared del carro, que se enciende y apaga con sólo abrir y cerrar la cajita en que está la bombilla, tal como se usa en los carros dormitorios del Ferrocarril Mexicano que corre de México a Veracruz.

Agregado a los carros dormitorios va un carro comedor, del cual me dí cuenta a la mañana siguiente; y éste fué para mí una novedad, pues siempre que habíamos viajado en México, nos servían en el mismo Pullman, sobre unas mesitas que se adaptan entre los asientos.

El carro comedor, además de ser bastante elegante, está perfectamente atendido, por una especie de administrador blanco, y varios meseros o mozos negros, que atienden con solícita prontitud a los pasajeros: ¡hasta vajilla pequeña hay para los niños! Figúrate, tía, que a mis hermanitas Tarsila y Rojana las ponían sus sillas pequeñas, sus platitos, sus cubiertos diminutos, sus pequeños vasos, tazas chiquitas y hasta miniaturas de servilletas, que me hacían pensar en mis juegos de muñecas, que estarán llenándose de polvo en la Villa Olga, en Mixcoac.

Toda la noche y todo el día caminamos, cruzando en éste, que fué cuando me dí cuenta, un paisaje monótono, formándolo en su mayor parte, terrenos amarillentos, sin cultivo de ninguna clase, que cortaban de cuando en cuando, las estaciones que ninguna belleza traían con su presencia.

San Antonio, Texas, que es una ciudad de importancia, de la que he leído algo, es la más importante de Houston a "El Paso"; pero ni la estación ví, porque por ella pasamos al amanecer, y yo iba profundamente dormida.

Sólo una cosa ví con verdadero regocijo, adelante de la estación "Del Río": el Bravo del Norte a cuya márgen caminamos largo rato: su aguas cenagosas y rápidas, señalaban el límite de mi Patria, representada aquí por ásperas rocas negruscas inconmovibles, ante el fuego del sol, sin un árbol, sin una gente; como si árboles y gentes quisiera ocultarse a los estragos de la guerra y del incendio.

A las diez de la noche, entraba nuestro tren a la ciudad de El Paso.

Olga Beatriz.

Tía Ciria:

El catorce de Julio fué el primer día que pasamos en El Paso. Abrí una de las ventanas de nuestro departamento en el Hotel Sheldon, cuyo frente da a la pequeña plaza y procuré orientarme: al frente, la calle de San Francisco, con una variedad de aspectos, desde la elegantes joyería con que empieza, hasta los lotes sin construir al final. A la derecha una gran tienda de ropa y el edifico "Anson Mills" que es el más alto de El Paso.

Este edificio fué constuído en el lugar en que se estableció la primera casa que hubo de este lado del ío, en tiempo de la dominación española, según supe después, por una inscripción que leí a la entrada y que dice:: **"On this spot then—near the river—opposite the ancient—City of Paso del Norte—Juan María Ponce de León—the first settler—on this side built this house in 1827".**[1]

Este solar fué adquirido por el general americano Anson Mills en 1857 y hasta hace unos cuantos años levantó el actual edificio, al cual le dió su nombre. Este general vive todavía.

En la misma pequeña plaza están las oficinas de "El Paso Herald" uno de los dos periódicos en inglés, diarios, que aquí se publican, una librería, el Hotel Mc-Coy, y en la esquina de la calle del Paso, las oficinas de un Banco. Esto fué lo primero que ví.

Olvidaba un detalle de nuestra llegada, que puede ser de utilidad

---

1. En este lugar, entonces cerca del río, frente a la antigua ciudad de Paso del Norte Juan María Ponce de León, el primer colono en este lado, construyó su casa en 1827.

a los viajero: al salir de la estación, numerosos automóviles, simétrica-
mente formados, esperaban a los pasajeros, los chauffeurs gritan invi-
tando a tomarlos, por cincuenta centavos por persona, rumbo a
cualquier hotel. Nos dirigimos a uno; pero el chauffeur codicioso insistía
en cobrar hasta por Rosana, niña de dieciocho meses; y mientras sobre
eso se hablaba, llegó un tranvía y lo tomamos: unas cuantas calles
recorrimos y llegamos al Hotel. Nos costó el asunto quince centavos,
en vez de veinte reales!

Se me ocurre, en vista de esto, dar un consejo a los viajeros: no
hay que tomar en la estación automóviles de ninguna clase; debe
esperarse un tranvía, todos van alkc entro y sólo cuesta cinco centavos
y tiene uno derecho a trasbordarse a otro tranvía, sin pagar nada extra,
con sólo pedir al conductor unos boletos que se llaman "transfer."

Mientras vestían a mis hermanitas, salí del hotel para dar vuelta
a la cuadra: atrás de él se encuentra el Correo, edificio de piedra en su
base; y de tabique el resto. Se encuentran las oficinas en el entresuelo,
al que se asciende por dos escaleras, una para cada calle, pues ocupa
una esquina; escaleras de piedra bastante anchas aunque muy paradas,
de manera que es molesto ascender por ellas. El conjunto del edifidico
es agradable.

Al Oriente del hotel está la plaza de San Jacinto, que es un jardín,
en el centro del cual hay un espacio circular cercado, en el que existen
dos grandes cocodrilos que son la admiración de todos los transeúntes.
Junto a ellos, y formando contraste, hay unas tortugas pequeñas, que
parece que ya se habituaron con tran tremenda compañía.

En este mismo jardín hay una enorme asta bandera en la que
ondea a una gran altura, el pabellón de las estrellas.

Sobre una gruta artificial, se encuentra un pequeño cañón de
recuerdos históricos para los nativos del Paso y junto a él un aviso en
el cual ofrecen cinco pesos de gratificación a todo aquel que aprehenda
al que destruya el jardín en algo y lo compruebe debidamente.

De manera que aquí todos los transeúntes se vigilan unos a otros y hasta ahora no he sabido que alguno se haya ganado los cinco pesos; o lo que es lo mismo, nadie destruye en lo más mínimo esta propiedad pública.

Aquí, como en Houston y creo que en todas las ciudades americanas, está prohibido escupir en los lugares públicos, bajo penas severas para evitar la propagación de enfermedades contagiosas, de manera que hay en este jardín su aviso respectivo en inglés y en español, para que todo el mundo se entere.

Volví al Hotel en busca del desayuno,m y al atravesar la calle, se me acercó un turba de papeleros voceando los periódicos de la mañana y entre ellos "El Imparcial" de México, que me hizo pensar en mi Patria querida y sobre todo, en mi casa da Mixcoac, que tan lejos estaba de mí.

En el Lobby del Hotel compré, siguiendo mi costumbre, una colección de tarjetas postales de El Paso y un plano, mis usuales pertrechos para conocer cuanto haya de bueno en la ciudad.

Olga Beatriz

✛ A Vuela Pájaro ✛

Tía Ciria:

Lee se llama el chauffeur de un poderoso automóvil que alquilamos para conocer la ciudad; y no es un hombre vulgar, sabe historia, cuenta anécdotas y refiere episodios más o menos curiosos de los lugares que enseña.

El primer día nos propusimos darle un vistazo a toda la ciudad a vuela máquina; así es que cómodamente instalados en el auto tripulado por Lee, salimos temprano del hotel y a correr por este Paso.

A la primera calle íbamos a cruzar la vía férrea cuando lentamente descendieron ante nosotros, unas largas tiras de madera roja, enclavadas en unas pequeñas columnas de fierro y no pudimos seguir adelante. Lee me explicó, por conductor de mi papá.

¿Vé usted, niña, esa torrecita de madera amarilla y roja, que está a la orilla de la vía? Dentro de ella, véalo usted, hay un hombre que por medio de una palanca, que tiene en este momento entre las manos, hace bajar esas tiras de madera que cubren las calles, y otras pequeñas que cubren la banqueta. En las tiras vea usted lo que se lee "**Safety First Stop—Look, Listen,**" lo que indica que debe uno salvarse ante todo y para ello, "detenerse, ver y escuchar"; porque se acerca un tren y es peligroso el paso; pero ya que además de advertirle, impide por completo el paso. Gracias a esto, continuó, no hay desgracias frecuentes; y no debía haberlas nunca, pero hay gentes que al llegar aquí no se detienen, ni ven, ni escuchan, sino que pasando debajo de esas tiras de madera, atraviesan la triple vía que aquí hay y suelen dejar su cuerpo hecho papilla entre los rieles.

Con velocidad de relámpago pasó ante nosotros una locomotora remolcando sesenta carros. Esta fué otra novedad para mí: las máquinas son enormes y deben tener una potencia tal, que esta que ví (y después se ha repetido el hecho) llevaba, tía, sesenta carros cargados hasta los topes.

Cuando el tren pasó, se levantaron lentamente las tiras de madera y como avalancha, pasaron la vía, y nosotros también, como éllos, varios automóviles, carros, bicicletas, motocicletas y como ochenta gentes que el paso del tren había detenido de uno y otro lado en su rápido ir y venir.

"Hay en Estados Unidos," agregó Lee, mientras hacía pitar el silvato del automóvil y cruzábamos la vía, una gran asociación que aquí, como en todas partes, tiene sus delegados, que por todos los medios posibles: vistas de cinematógrafo, conferencias, avisos, artículos en los periódicos, pláticas en las iglesias y advertencias personales, tienden a disminuir los accidentes desgraciados en que la imprevisión del individuo tiene la principal culpa; de manera que por donde quiera se tropezará usted con el `**Safety First**' que es su lema, o lo que es lo mismo `la salvación primero', es decir, que antes de cualquier interés o asunto en la tierra, debe evitarse un accidente desgraciado."

Llegamos al jardín Cleveland, que es uno de los más bonitos que hay en El Paso, ciudad en verdad, pobre de jardines, si se compara con cualquiera ciudad mexicana. En el centro de este jardín está la Biblioteca Pública, de la cual te hablaré después, basta por ahora decirte que su entrada está formada por un hall o terraza a cuyo frente se levantan cuatro gruesas columnas, dándole a la fachada gran semejanza con el templo de Diana, de Éfeso, que ví en mi Manual de Historia Universal. Se llega a esta terraza por una amplia y cómoda escalera de piedra.

Dimos vuelta después por el propio jardín Cleveland y pasamos frente al templo masónico, edificio de siete pisos, construido de cemento y ladrillo rojo obscuro. Frente a la esquina Sur-este del jardín habíamos ya pasado el edificio de la Asociación de Jóvenes, cuya fachada sólo tiene de bonito una serie de arcos concéntricos que sirven de entrada, el resto muestra solidez; pero no belleza.

Por una calle bastante pendiente, llegamos a Sunset-Heights, que es un barrio de El Paso, en donde se encuentran indudablemente, las casas más bonitas de la población.

El terreno en que se asienta la ciudad no es plano, sino en su parte central y lo que se le ha ido quitando al río (y de paso a nosotros los mexicanos) de manera que la ciudad ha ido ascendiendo las lomas y los cerros cercanos, que en la imposibilidad de nivelarlos han construído sobre ellos, de manera que hay casas arriba y otras más abajo, todas de distintos planos, lo que le da al conjunto cierta originalidad y gran belleza. Sunset Heights así está, y como aquí, ya te lo dije antes, las casas están aisladas, es decir, no va una pegada a la otra, sino que cada una tiene libres sus cuatro lados; esta diferencia de nivel las hace aparecer en conjunto como los nacimientos de Noche Buena.

En el centro de Sunset Heights hay un bien cuidado jardín de forma romboidal, en el cual desembocan las avenidas Porfirio Díaz, Lawton, Upson, Prospect y West Boulevard; todas ellas con grandes, hermosas y elegantes residencias.

Nos detuvimos un poco frente al parque, y siguiendo luego por la venida Prospect llegamos a la calle High, la cual seguimos en línea recta hasta la Escuela Preparatoria (High School) y luego por una serie de calles zig-zag pasamos por el barrio Franklin Heigts y luego High-land Park hasta llegar a las últimas casas, y de allí regresamos por Manhathan Heights (otro barrio), y entramos a la calle de Montana, una de las más modernas, la cual seguimos en más de veinticinco cuadras, pues es muy larga y bien pavimentada, hasta North Oregon, que nos llevó al hotel, mareados de aquel desfile de casas y calles, y púseme tranquilamente a ordenar mis notas para escribir después estos renglones.

Olga Beatriz

✛ Incomprensible Castellano ✛

Nos instalamos.

Nuestra casa era un juguete, estilo misión, acabado de hacer: cinco piezas y baño, además del correspondiente "**Sleeping Porch,**" en donde cómodamente instalamos o más bien dicho ya estaban instalados tres catres. Los muebles no eran muchos, pero los existentes nuevos enteramente y entre ellos un magnífico piano, que media hora después de instalados dejó escapar, a impulsos de mis manos, las siempre bellas notas del Himno Nacional mexicano, que seguramente, por la primera vez desde que salió de la fábrica, estremecían el cordaje de sus sonoros pulmones. Sobre él extendí, a guisa de cubierta, nuestra bandera, para hacerme la ilusión de que se había realizado en tierras extranjeras una conquista mexicana.

Sobre la mesa del comedor, una maceta en el centro, dejaba caer a sus lados un espárrago que la dueña de la casa nos había recomendadado como un ojo de la cara. ¡Y pensar que en la Villa Olga de Mixcoac le hacemos tanto caso!

La casa tenía teléfono, dos estufas, una de gas y otra para leña, suficiente vajilla, trastos para la cocina, y en fin, cuanto puede necesitarse para pasar la vida sin incomodidades; en una palabra, nada había superfluo; pero nada faltaba tampoco, y todo esto por cuarenta y cinco pesos al mes ¿verdad que no es tan caro, tía?

Entre las numerosas mujeres que llegaron en busca de colocación, aceptamos a una que aseguró saber cuanto hubiera en materia de cocina; pero en realidad, poco sabía la pobre; pero en cambio, aprendí con ella el dialecto que hablan aquí la mayor parte de los mexicanos que ya tienen mucho tiempo en ésta.

Porque debes saber, tía Ciria, que no es tan fácil entender el castellano de los mexicanos de Texas, los cuales, en contacto con los americanos, han mexicanizado muchas palabras inglesas y han anglicanizado muchas castellanas, de manera que su dialecto, es una mezcla de español e inglés, incorrectos los dos, mal pronunciados los dos e incomprensibles en verdad.

Te citaré un ejemplo: un día faltó la criada en la mañana y cuando por la tarde llegó y le pregunté la causa de su falta, me contestó en la siguiente forma, que supongo ha de ser difícil que traduzcas:

"Venía yo de la **Esmelda ayer**; y pedí en el **carro** un **trance** para ir al **Dipo**, en donde me habían dicho que había una **marqueta**, y yo necesitaba comprar unas **mechas**, y ver si había un calentón barato, para el cual ya tengo bastante leña en la **yardita**; pero cuando ya iba llegando, se descompuso el **traque** y tuve que esperar, dirigiéndome a la casa de **la familia** López, de Chihuahua. Allí los **babis** habían rotó un paquete de **espauda;** de ese que se usa en los **bísquetes**; y me pidió la señora prestado un **daime,** para comprar otro, y como yo no tenía más que ese, tuve que hacer el viaje a pie, y me puse mala, por eso no vine temprano."

¿Entendiste? ¿Verdad que no? Pues allá va la explicación: **esmelda,** le llaman aquí al barrio en donde está la fundición de metales que en inglés se llama **Smelter.** Carro le llaman al tranvía, porque en inglés se dice **car. Dipo,** es incorrección de **depot,** que en inglés es estación del ferrocarril. **Trance** es un boleto que dan en los tranvías para trasbordarse a otro tranvía sin pagar, del cual ya te hablé en otra carta, cuyo boleto en inglés se dice **transfer.**

Marqueta dicen en vez de mercado, que en inglés es **market; mechas,** son cerillos, y lo han tomado del inglés **matches,** que significa cerillos. Calentón es un barbarismo castellano, pues lo usan en vez de **calentador,** especie de estufa portátil que se usa en el interior de las casas en invierno. **Yardita** es un diminuto mexicano de la palabra inglesa **yard** que significa patio, corral. **Traque** le llaman a la vía de tranvías que en inglés se dice **track.** Porcha es la palabra **porch,** castellanizada, y son esos portales de que te hablé en mi anterior. **Babis** es disparate de la palabra inglesa **babies,** niños. **Espauda,** usan en vez de **powder** levadura en polvo y **bísquetes,** es mexicanización de **biscuits,** que son pastelitos o pequeños panes. **Daime** lo usan los mexicanos en vez del inglés **dime,** que se pronuncia **daim** y es el nombre de las monedas de plata de a diez *centavos.*

Ya con estas explicaciones podrás traducir el incomprensible castellano de Carlota, (que así se llama la criada,) que es el mismo que usan la mayor parte de los trabajadores y servidumbre mexicana. ¡Americanos y compatriotas, necesitan intérprete para entenderles!

Tu sobrina.

Olga.

Letters (Spanish)

Arce, Miguel. *¡Ladrona¡* San Antonio: Casa Editorial Lozano, 1925.

Bruce-Novoa, Juan. "*La Prensa* and the Chicano Community." *Americas Review* 17, no. 3–4 (Fall/Winter 1989): 150–59.

———. *Retrospace: Collected Essays on Chicano Literature.* Houston: Arte Público Press, 1980.

Castillo, Adelaida R. Del. *Between Borders: Essays on Mexicana/Chicana History.* Encino, Calif.: Floricanto Press, 1990.

García, Mario T. *Desert Immigrants: The Mexican of El Paso, 1980–1920.* New Haven: Yale University Press, 1981.

———. *Mexican American: Leadership, Ideology, and Identity 1930–1960.* New Haven: Yale University Press, 1989.

García, Richard A. *Rise of the Mexican-American Middle Class: San Antonio, 1929–1941.* College Station: Texas A&M Press, 1991.

González, Alfredo. *Carranza.* San Antonio: Casa Editorial Lozano, 1928.

Hart, John Mason. *Revolutionary Mexico: The Coming and Process of the Mexican Revolution.* Berkeley and Los Angeles: University of California Press, 1987.

Hernández, Guillermo E. "El México de fuera: notas para historia cultural." *Crítica: A Journal of Critical Essays* 1, no. 3 (Fall 1986): 60–80.

Hernández-Tovar, Inés. "Sara Estela Ramírez: The Early Twentieth Century Texas-Mexican Poet." Ph.D. diss., University of Houston, 1984.

Henderson, Peter V. N. *Mexican Exiles in the Borderlands 1910–1913.* Monograph No. 58. El Paso: Texas Western Press, 1979.

Hinojosa, Féderico Allen. *El México de Afuera y su reintegración a la patria.* San Antonio: Artes Gráficas, 1940.

Leal, Luis. "Six Pre-Chicana Writers." *Encuentro* 8, no. 3 (Spring Quarter 1984): 2–3.

———. "The Spanish-Language Press: Function and Use." *Americas Review* 17, no. 3–4 (Fall–Winter 1989): 157–62.

Lomas, Clara. "Mexican Precursors of Chicana Feminist Writings." In *Multiethnic Literature of the United States* Edited by Cordelia Candelaria. Boulder, Colo.: University of Colorado Press, 1989.

Onofre, Stefano di. "*La Prensa* of San Antonio and Its Literary Page, 1913–1915." Ph.D. diss., University of California, Los Angeles, 1983.

Parle, Dennis J. "The Novels of the Mexican Revolution Published by the Casa Editorial Lozano." *Americas Review* 17, no. 3–4 (Fall/Winter 1989): 163–68.

Rebolledo, Diana Tey. "Las Escritoras: Romances and Realities." In *Pasó por aquí*. Edited by Erlinda Gonzales-Berry. Albuquerque: University of New Mexico Press, 1989.

Reyes, José Asención. *El automóvil gris*. San Antonio: Casa Editorial Lozano, 1922.

———. *Heraclio Bernal: El Rayo de Sinoloa*. San Antonio: Casa Editorial Lozano, 1920.

Rio-McMillan, Nora. "A Biography of a Man and His Newspaper." *Americas Review* 17, no. 3–4 (Fall–Winter 1989): 136–49.

Robe, Stanley L. *Azuela and the Mexican Underdogs*. Berkeley and Los Angeles: University of California Press, 1979.

San Miguel, Guadalupe, Jr. *"LET ALL OF THEM TAKE HEED": Mexican Americans and the Campaign for Educational Equality in Texas, 1910–1981*. Austin: University of Texas Press, 1987.

Soto, Shirlene. *Emergence of the Modern Mexican Woman: Her Participation in Revolution and Struggle for Equality, 1910–1940*. Denver: Arden Press, 1990.

Torres, Teodoro. *Pancho Villa: Una vida de romance y tragedia*. San Antonio: Casa Editorial Lozano, 1924.